THE REIGN OF HENRY VIII

David Starkey is the prize-winning author of *Elizabeth*, a number one bestseller in both hardback and paperback, and, most recently, *Six Wives: The Queens of Henry VIII*. The associated TV series on Queen Elizabeth I – which he devised, wrote and presented – topped the Channel Four ratings. Even more successful was his TV series, *The Six Wives of Henry VIII*, which was watched by 4.5 million viewers and nominated for a BAFTA award. His previous TV series, *David Starkey's Henry VIII*, won the Indie Documentary Award 2002, while *Elizabeth* was warded the biography prize by WH Smith.

Historian, commentator and broadcaster on both TV and radio, Dr Starkey is Bye Fellow of Fitzwilliam College, Cambridge.

For further information, and details of forthcoming projects, see www.davidstarkey.com.

ALSO BY DAVID STARKEY

This Land of England

*Revolution Reassessed: Revisions in the History of
Tudor Government and Administration*

*The English Court from the Wars of the Roses
to the Civil War*

*Rivals in Power: The Lives and Letters
of the Great Tudor Dynasties*

Henry VIII: A European Court in England

The Inventory of King Henry VIII

Elizabeth: Apprenticeship

Six Wives: The Queens of Henry VIII

David Starkey

THE REIGN OF HENRY VIII

PERSONALITIES AND POLITICS

VINTAGE BOOKS
London

Published by Vintage 2002

10

First published in Great Britain in 1985 by
George Philip

Vintage
Random House, 20 Vauxhall Bridge Road,
London SW1V 2SA

www.vintage-books.co.uk

Addresses for companies within The Random House Group
Limited can be found at: www.randomhouse.co.uk/offices.htm

The Random House Group Limited Reg. No. 954009

A CIP catalogue record for this book
is available from the British Library

ISBN 9780099445104

The Random House Group Limited supports The Forest Stewardship
Council® (FSC®), the leading international forest-certification organisation.
Our books carrying the FSC label are printed on FSC®-certified paper.
FSC is the only forest-certification scheme supported by the leading
environmental organisations, including Greenpeace. Our
paper procurement policy can be found at
www.randomhouse.co.uk/environment

Typeset by SX Composing DTP, Rayleigh, Essex

Printed and bound in Great Britain by Clays Ltd, St Ives PLC

To J.O., who has monarchical aspirations too

CONTENTS

Illustration Sources and Acknowledgements

18. Artist unknown, William Cary (Private Collection).
19. Henry VIII's letter to Wolsey (British Library).
20. Artist unknown, the Field of Cloth of Gold (reproduced by kind permission of HM the Queen).
21. Artist unknown, Battle of Pavia (reproduced by kind permission of HM the Queen).
22. Hans Holbein, Queen Anne Boleyn (reproduced by kind permission of HM the Queen).
23. Gerlack Flicke, Thomas Cranmer (National Portrait Gallery).
24. Hans Holbein, Sir John Russell, Earl of Bedford (reproduced by kind permission of HM the Queen).
25. Hans Holbein, Thomas Cromwell (National Portrait Gallery).
26. Artist unknown, Stephen Gardiner (Trinity College, Cambridge).
27. Artist unknown, Garter procession of 1534, from the Black Book of the Order of the Garter (reproduced by permission of the Dean and Canons of Windsor).
28. Hans Holbein, Sir William Butts (Isabella Stewart Gardner Museum, Boston).
29. Artist unknown, Sir Anthony Browne (National Portrait Gallery).
30. School of Holbein, Sir Anthony Denny (Courtauld Institute).
31. Henry VIII reading in his Bedchamber (British Library).
32. (?) William Scrots, Catherine Parr (National Portrait Gallery).
33/34. Hans Holbein, Sir Philip and Lady Hoby (reproduced by kind permission of HM the Queen).
35. Artist unknown, woodcut of the burning of Anne Ascue (Mansell Collection).
36. Henry Howard, Earl of Surrey (Arundel Castle, courtesy of the Duke of Norfolk).
37. Hans Holbein, Anne of Cleves (Mansell Collection).
38. Attributed to Guillim Scrots, Sir William Paget (National Portrait Gallery, London).
39. The last page of Henry VIII's will (The Public Record Office).
40. Artist unknown, allegory of Edward VI's regime (National Portrait Gallery).

FOREWORD

Books, to their writers at least, are rather like children. This is my eldest, and so has a special place in my affection. I also enjoyed writing it. Indeed I can still remember my pleasure as I discovered, for the first time, how to forge the brute materials of historical fact and argument into a satisfying aesthetic pattern. Finally, and most importantly, people enjoyed reading it. One reviewer enjoyed it so much that he called it a 'champagne cocktail' and lamented that it was so short!

This new edition will be an opportunity for readers, old and new, to take another sip of the glass and to treat it as an aperitif to my more recent, bigger books.

D.S.
Highbury, London
July 2002

PREFACE TO THE ORIGINAL EDITION

This little book owes a great deal to two men: Professor G. R. Elton and the late Hugh Murray Baillie. I read Professor Elton's books at school; was taught by him as an undergraduate and supervised by him as a research student. Subsequently we have sometimes come to disagree. But the training he gave me in administrative history remains the foundation of my historical skills, such as they are, and provides the point of departure of the present book.

I met Hugh Murray Baillie much later. But his influence was no less strong. The warmest and the least insular of men, he taught me three things. That structure was not simply a matter of institutions, but of feelings and belief; that history must be international and comparative; and that paintings and buildings are as important historical evidence as documents.

A book as short as this is not perhaps the best way of paying two such heavy debts. But those who know me well will be surprised that it has appeared at all. That it has is due to two other people: Nett Capsey, who has typed it, and the editor, Lydia Greeves, who has cajoled and encouraged the writer in equal measures and to equal effect!

David Starkey
Highbury, London
June 1985

INTRODUCTION

WHY WRITE ANOTHER BOOK on Henry VIII? Henry VIII is the King whose shape everybody remembers. He is also the King whose life everybody seems to have written. This is not another one. Only new evidence could justify that. Instead it is a new approach.

Henry, who has been tackled in isolation by his multitude of biographers, was in fact almost never alone. He was surrounded, twenty-four hours a day, by the small group of intimates and personal attendants who made up the staff of his Privy Chamber. They organized his daily life; kept him amused as his companions in the joust, hunt and revel; and acted as the land-line between the King and the formal machinery of the government that Henry controlled yet never ran in detail. These men, intermarried, interbred and close-knit even in their mutual feuding, were supremely well-placed to rig politics and patronage for their own benefit. Just how much influence they exercised over the King cannot now be finally determined. But often they were important and sometimes decisive. And at the most crucial moments of the reign: factions in the Privy Chamber destroyed Anne Boleyn; frustrated the 'Catholic' reaction of the 1540s, and, by doctoring Henry's will, prepared the way for the full-blooded Protestantism of his son's reign.

So this book is not about Henry VIII. It is about the great game of politics over which he presided. The first chapter

lays down the ground rules: it describes the King's character; outlines the structure of politics, and discusses contemporary analyses of the role of the courtier. There then
follows a blow-by-blow account of the game: 'a king's
game, and for the more part played on scaffolds', as More,
who himself played hard and lost, called it. And periodi-
cally we look up from the gore and the detail and ask why
it all mattered.

It mattered and still matters for several reasons. Most
simply, it makes an excellent story: there's rich incident,
bizarre detail, including the King's toilet habits, and a marvellous cast of hitherto unknown characters, ranging from
the Vicar of Hell to the King's Pig. But it cuts more deeply
as well. It introduces a heroine into the age of Tudor Kings:
Anne Boleyn, a sixteenth-century woman who knew what
she wanted; got it, and eventually paid the price. And it
presents a new view of the King and the most important
event of the reign: the Reformation. Henry was not the
archetypal strong King. He was not weak either, but he
was manipulable – and through his strongest defences, his
suspiciousness and his refusal ever to give his confidence
completely, which offered coigns of vantage to intrigue
and backbiting. While the Reformation was not simply a
great popular movement; it was also the work of a court
faction. It is possible, though unlikely, that the popular
Reformation could have succeeded on its own, but the outcome would have been unrecognizably different.

Finally, the argument of the book even makes a contribution, at least by implication, to the comparative study of
government. It is, of course, about the past, that 'other
country' of long ago and far away. But strip off the local
detail – the cloth of gold on the one hand and the heading
block on the other – and its subject becomes both universal and immediately relevant. Henry VIII, like any prime
minister, president, or company chairman today who is

worth their salt, established a managerial style. This created both difficulties and opportunities for his servants. And their response would be familiar to any ambitious politician or executive now. In fact, to transfer from Tudor Whitehall to the modern White House requires little more than a change of clothes!

I

THE NATURE OF POLITICS

'THE PRINCE IS THE LIFE, the head and the authority of all things that be done in the realm of England.' And no king has more completely fulfilled Sir Thomas Smith's dictum than Henry VIII. The impress of his massive personality lies heavily on all aspects of his reign, and on its politics in particular.

But it is easy to be deceived by the outward show of Henry's character. To all appearances, he stands as the very model of a strong king. Certainly this is how he saw himself; more importantly, it is how Holbein, the greatest of his court painters, chose to represent him. And the image (as was intended) has been almost universally accepted: by contemporaries, by the King's own daughter Elizabeth I, and by succeeding generations, including most professional historians.

Nor was the image wholly false. Physically Henry fitted the part to perfection. He was tall and well-built, and even the massive fat of his later years only made him the more overwhelming. Mentally, too, he had many of the qualities of a born leader. He was intelligent; his memory was good and his eye for detail sharp. He was a shrewd judge of men and had a flair for self-projection and propaganda. Moreover, he was both ruthless and selfish, while his staggering self-righteousness made him proof against doubts and the dark night of the soul.

But all this was undercut by other, less impressive traits. First there was Henry's addiction to sport in all its forms: jousting, hunting, tennis. This was not altogether a bad thing of course, and only a handful of wimp humanists thought that it was. They, like reforming schoolmasters who feel that too much time is devoted to organized sport and too much prestige gained from it, were satirical about Henry's 'converting hunting into martyrdom'. (Though they took good care to keep their satire safely in Latin.) Nearly everybody who mattered took a different line, however. For even a cultivated and sensitive gentleman, like the poet, Sir Thomas Wyatt, hunting and hawking were the mainstay of an agreeable country existence, with books saved up for 'foul weather'. While for ordinary chaps, like Sir Anthony Browne or his half-brother, Sir William Fitzwilliam, it was a master passion. That the King shared it was a bond of union. And not only in the field. For when Henry had 'had good sport, he will talk thereof three or four days after'. Similarly with jousting. Granted it was dangerous (Henry escaped death by a miracle in 1524), and that it could lead to excessive familiarity with his sporting partners, who occasionally 'played such light touches with him that they forgot themselves'. It also, on the positive side, gave a King who had never been bloodied on the field of battle the necessary war-like credentials. For the chronicler Edward Hall, and for most of Henry's subjects, every spear he broke in the lists was a 'martial feat' and every course he ran a 'service to Mars'.

The real problem in fact was time. Many a long, lazy month was spent on horseback, as in 1526 when, as Hall laconically noted, 'because all this summer this King took his pastime in hunting, . . . nothing happened worthy to be written of'. And even in an ordinary court day Henry was usually willing to apply himself seriously to business only in the mid-morning while he heard mass, and again late at night after supper. That is not to say that he was simply idle, and certainly that he was not interested. About heraldry and genealogy, for example, he was an expert. And these mattered when claims to estates, offices and whole kingdoms depended on disentangling dynastic niceties. His theological learning, though unsystematic, was real too (and probably not all that uncommon among an English upper class that prided itself on a self-conscious piety). He delighted in things mechanical; would pore over building plans for hours and designed arms and fortifications himself. Where he fell down was in the application to routine in which his father had excelled. He could scarcely be bothered to look at accounts, let alone check them; he would read nothing more than a short letter, and often not even that; while writing, as he himself said, was 'to me . . . somewhat tedious and painful'. So a whole letter in his own hand was a portent; and even extracting his signature took time and art. None of this made him a cipher. He had secretaries and attendants to do his reading and writing for him, and councillors to cope with the detailed execution of policy and finance. But even when his whole energies were involved it put him at one remove from events: he saw and heard indeed, but through the eyes and ears of others.

Thomas Wolsey, Henry's chief councillor and the man who understood the King best, of course realized all this and always had a special carping distrust of the royal Secretary, whoever he was and however loyal. His fear was not only that the Secretary might abuse his strategic position, but that Henry might take a sudden fancy to one so near him. For the King was prone to lightning enthusiasms, about people and things. An incident in 1521 – itself trivial enough – shows the cast of his mind particularly clearly. The practice of English kings was to sign their letters at the top and seal them with the signet beneath. The French King, on the other hand, signed his letters at the bottom and used no seal. Henry had received such a letter from Francis I of France and suddenly determined that it should be a 'precedent' for his future correspondence. Accordingly, he threw his Secretary, Richard Pace, into a fit of anxiety by refusing absolutely to 'superscribe . . . or put wax' on letters to the Emperor and the Regent of the Netherlands. Soon, of course, the novelty wore off and things drifted back to their accustomed pattern, with little harm done, apart from driving poor Pace another few steps towards his eventual nervous collapse. But when people were the subject of Henry's enthusiasms it was another matter. Henry was Wolsey's 'loving master'; Henry Norris was 'the best beloved of the King'; Anne Boleyn 'mine own darling'. Here again the enthusiasm burned out, but destructively. Like a child grown tired of a toy, the King broke each sometime beloved in pieces: Wolsey was hounded to his death; Norris and Anne were executed. And they were but three of many:

> For how many servants did he advance in haste . . . and with the change of his fancy ruined again . . .? To how many others of more desert gave he abundant flowers, from whence to gather honey, and in the end of harvest burned them in the hive?

And as with men so with measures. Most striking is the question of religion. Henry was to break with Rome on purely political grounds. He wanted to divorce Catherine of Aragon and marry Anne Boleyn. The Pope would not, could not, agree. So the Pope had to go. But the breach with Rome, and still more the means by which it was achieved, opened the Pandora's box of religious

4

controversy that we call the Reformation. And not even Henry VIII, however hard he pushed, could close it again. Anne Boleyn and her allies, such as Thomas Cromwell, were interested in the new 'evangelical' approach to religion. This emphasized the redeeming power of Christ's words in the gospels, as opposed to the ritual and 'smells and bells' of late medieval Catholicism. And many that Anne and Cromwell patronized went further and challenged the actual theological basis of Catholicism. In so doing they drew indifferently on the new Continental heresies of Martin Luther and on the old native tradition of dissent known as Lollardy. Both rejected the idea of a priesthood which mediated between God and man by re-enacting the miracle of the mass, thus transforming the elements of bread and wine into the very body and blood of Christ; and both emphasized instead the direct meeting of Christ and the believer, in conscience rather than in church, and through faith rather than ritual. The English Church had been well armed against Lollardy and the old machinery was turned against the new heresies as well. And with a new energy once Wolsey's wavering hand was removed and people such as Stephen Gardiner, the Bishop of Winchester, took over. These distinct religious positions within the political élite were well understood by contemporaries, who labelled them 'new' and 'old' respectively.

Henry's own position in all this was wilfully complicated. Certainly the old view that he was essentially orthodox, 'a Catholic without the Pope', must go. Quite quickly he challenged the divine ordination of priesthood; and by the end he was openly talking of replacing the mass with a communion service. But equally the development of his religious thought was erratic and crab-like. It was also subject to a bewildering variety of pressures: from the mainstream of foreign policy and domestic politics, to the often violent cross-eddies produced by his lust, vanity,

greed, and most of the other deadly sins, which he practised in generous measure. The result was that the course
of religious policy rather resembles a big dipper: the 'new'
rose with Anne Boleyn and trembled in the balance when
she fell; the 'old', or much of it, was triumphantly restored
in 1539 only to wilt when its principal champions, Stephen
Gardiner, the Bishop of Winchester, and the Howards,
were systematically rooted out in the last weeks of the
reign.

As they were, the Imperial Ambassador wrung his hands
whilst the French cautiously rejoiced. Religion and foreign
policy were closely connected and the latter was as helter-
skelter as the former. One moment Henry was swearing
life-long amity with his 'good brother' Francis I of France;
the next, and occasionally indeed at the same time, he was
pledging eternal alliance with the Emperor Charles V, the
ruler of Germany, the Netherlands and Spain. Bluff, in
short, King Hal might have looked, but bluff and
straightforward his leadership was not. His fluctuating
enthusiasms and bewildering changes of front offered
everyone of ambition the hope that some day the sun of
favour would shine on them. Whilst his disinclination to
business and devotion to pleasure seemed to provide many
means to bring that happy day closer. Maybe indeed Henry
was an almost human Shiva, the lord of the dance, who
'took all the decisions' and made and unmade at his
absolute will. But I doubt it. Just as his behaviour provoked
intrigue, so surely did intrigue affect his behaviour.
Contemporaries thought that it did and acted as though it
did. We would be wise to follow them.

So Henry's personality shaped a politics of intrigue, even
manipulation. But not in a vacuum. For England, as
James I asserted a century later, was a kingdom 'settled in
civility and policy'. Already there were institutions of
government and a system of law that were both old and

deeply-entrenched. For instance, Henry could not simply say, like the Red Queen in *Alice in Wonderland*, 'off with his head!' Instead the accused had to be condemned by due process of law. Trials of course were rigged. But rigging took much effort and could go embarrassingly wrong. The limitations imposed by the nature of the administrative machine were subtler, but probably cut even deeper. All this ruled out autocracy, even for a King as self-willed as Henry occasionally showed himself to be. More importantly in everyday terms it gave shape to the disparate influences operating on the King: in other words, working in conjunction with the royal personality, it created a structure of politics.

In English government, apart from the King himself, there were two main foci of power: the administration, centring on the Council, and the royal household or court. These two power centres had been identified in the fifteenth century by Sir John Fortescue, the author of *The Governance of England*, who had distinguished between the constitutionally acceptable – indeed necessary – role of the King's Council, and what he saw as the illicit influence of the 'men of his Chamber [or] of his household, . . . which cannot counsel him'.

The administration consisted of the Exchequer, which usually controlled finance, and a complex secretariat which was made up of the offices of the three seals: the Great Seal, the Privy Seal and the Signet. These three seals passed the King's instructions to each other, to other government departments, and to the King's subjects. Till recently they had been supreme. But in the later fifteenth century they were being elbowed aside by a more modern and much less formalized means of authenticating documents: the King's signature or sign manual. The two senior departments, the Exchequer and the Chancery, which dealt with the Great Seal, had their own permanent headquarters. The records of Chancery were kept in the Rolls Chapel in Chancery Lane, close by the lawyers of the Inns of Court who gave it much of its business; and the Exchequer had its own building by Westminster Hall. The Privy Seal and Signet, however, usually followed the King on his restless travels.

Ordinarily, the heads of these four departments – the Lord Treasurer, the Lord Chancellor, the Lord Privy Seal and the Secretary – were the most important and active members of the Council. But the Council, unlike the administrative departments, was not really an institution. Instead, its composition, size and even functions varied greatly from king to king. Sometimes, it was the real government; sometimes, it was almost impotent. More usually, however, there was a middle way in which it blended advisory, executive and judicial activities to make it the King's chief auxiliary in the running of his kingdom. This system – crudely and briefly described – had proved both flexible and durable, but it had two major defects: save for the Exchequer (which was in any case in full decline) there was little functional specialization among the various departments; nor, much more seriously, was there any formalized machinery for co-ordinating the work of government. That task, instead, was peculiarly the King's own.

The other centre of power was the royal court or household, which stood much nearer the King. Literally so. The administration was based in Westminster, and for half the year, during the legal terms when the Law Courts were in session, the Council normally met there as well. The King's itinerary was much more flexible. During the winter months he too tended to stay at palaces in or near London. But in the summer he would go on long hunting expeditions or 'progresses'. These took him deep into the countryside, to his own numerous palaces (Henry VIII had fifty-five by the end of his reign), or to the houses of favoured courtiers or councillors. For several months a year then, the King and most of the Council were widely separated geographically; his court or household was always with him, however. Its size varied of course. The full household, numbering hundreds if not thousands, could only be accommodated in the great palaces in-and-around London. In the progress time, on the other hand, the King's retinue could shrink to a handful, with even the Queen being left behind in some pleasant suburban retreat, like Greenwich.

But always the key figures of the household were there. Essentially they were the staff of the King's palace, and the internal organization of the household derived from the geography of the typical medieval palace. In this there were two functionally separate areas which met in the great hall. This had originally been a communal dining-room, in which the King feasted on the dais while his servants ate in the body of the hall. The body of the hall and the adjacent domestic offices of the kitchens and buttery etc. formed one area of the palace; the dais of the hall and the King's first-floor private apartment, or Chamber, formed the other. The first was the public, service area of the palace; the second was the private royal quarters. The servants of the first were grouped into one department of the royal household, under the Lord Steward, while the staff of the second made up the other under their head, the Lord Chamberlain. The two departments were known, respectively, as the Household (which was thus confusingly the name of both the whole court and of one department within it) and the Chamber, and corresponded to the 'downstairs' and 'upstairs' of the great household of the eighteenth or nineteenth centuries.

And, like the two worlds on either side of the green baize door, the Household and Chamber were very different. We can still get the feel of them in the surviving Tudor

9

buildings of Hampton Court. The service or household side lies to one side of the great hall. From the palace gardens its confusion of gables and pitched roofs looks like a medieval town and the impression is reinforced within by a maze of courtyards, arches and brick-vaulted passage-ways. At the centre lie the vast kitchens, a battery of serving hatches along one wall. These were strategically overseen by the Clerk of the Kitchen from his office with its split door. Around clustered specialized offices, like the Pastry, the Spicery and the Larder. In overall control was the high-powered committee of the senior accountants and managers of the Household, known as the Board of Green Cloth. The size of the buildings still impresses; even so it is important to get the scale right. The Household numbered hundreds and was by far the largest single institution in the country. So much so that in war, its chief administrator, the Cofferer, was a natural choice as head of the commissariat.

We are of course in no danger of underestimating the other department of the household. Beyond the richly carved door by the dais of the hall – nicely known as the King's threshold – was the Chamber. Here hung rich tapestries and stood sideboards heaped with plate. Guards, musicians, and attendants in silk and gold chains played their part in the great moments of the court day, when the King went to chapel, or dined, or received an ambassador in state. While a much smaller cast of servants, more highly favoured and still more magnificently dressed, attended on the King himself in his more private hours.

That, painted in gold, is a picture of a court as we all understand it. But the Chamber was more. It was a centre of power. Its upper servants were linchpins of government, both at the centre and on the periphery. They acted as the King's eyes and ears in the counties, in the army and in diplomacy. Moreover, thanks to their intimacy with the

King, they could exercise an immense influence on patronage, which was itself a fundamental key to power. Finally, they were the King's auxiliaries in those areas of government he chose to perform himself. Under Edward IV and Henry VII the chief financial officer of the Chamber, the Treasurer of the Chamber, displaced the Exchequer to become pay-master of the whole kingdom, while the King's Secretary was also a member of the department.

So that Council and court were important went without saying. Just how important, though, depended on the personality of the King. Henry VII, the first Tudor King, won the throne in 1485 when he defeated and killed Richard III in the battle at Bosworth. Trained in the rough school of penury, exile and insignificance, he had won power hardly and would never let it slip from him, even for a moment. This determination not to admit 'any near or full approach, either to his power or to his secrets' coloured his whole style of government. He kept key functions in his own hands – spending endless hours, for example, toiling over the books of the Treasurer of the Chamber, which characteristically were at once the accounts of his household and his kingdom. And when he had to delegate, he kept a firm rein on even the most trusted servants of his court and Council.

The Council was large and active. It had a major advisory role, and its various 'committees' or 'by-courts' were the key executive instruments of Henry VII's government. But despite this activity, it had no independent authority of its own. It gave advice only when the King asked and only on subjects he laid before it; while the 'by-courts' were not true committees of the Council as they reported back not to it but to the King, who alone defined their areas of activity and conferred their power. Henry, in fact, was not only his own Prime Minister and Treasurer, but his own Secretary of State as well.

11

Matters were much the same at court. This Henry VII maintained in great magnificence, as the symbol of the stability and strength of his regime. It was also required to work for its keep. Henry VII had come to the throne with a strong following of knights and gentlemen drawn from some of the best county families of the south-east. We think of Henry as 'Lancastrian', but the diverse political origins of his following tell a more complex story. Some of them had been the household knights of the Yorkist Edward IV; some were members of the affinity of the Woodvilles, the family of Edward IV's Queen; others were the friends and associates of Reginald Bray, who was right-hand man of Lady Margaret Beaufort, Henry Tudor's mother. What had brought this diverse group together was the violent usurpation of Edward IV's brother, Richard of Gloucester. Richard first disinherited and then murdered his nephews, the young Edward V and his brother, the heirs of Edward IV and Queen Elizabeth Woodville. This alienated much of the Yorkist establishment; it also gave Margaret Beaufort's son his chance. The first joint rising against Richard III, misleadingly known as Buckingham's Rebellion, took place in 1483 and was a dismal failure. Some of the leaders were executed; others fled to join Henry Tudor in Brittany. But all was vindicated with the triumph of Bosworth two years later.

So the leaders of this group had shared exile with Henry and fought with him on the field of battle. Thus cemented, the bonds endured for the whole reign. Men like Sir Thomas Lovell, Sir Richard Guildford and Sir Reginald Bray ran local government; held key administrative offices; were the dominant figures at court and turned the Order of the Garter into a private club. Their relations with each other were close; so were their relations with the King. Hard-working though Henry was, he was not without his pleasures. He enjoyed hunting, cards and shooting. And these men were his companions. But it was a companionship that had strict limits. Henry's pleasures were private; when it came to the public entertainments of the court, the jousts and revels, Henry carefully kept his distance. He never took part; instead he was only 'a princely and gentle spectator'. And he kept his distance institutionally too, by reforming the royal household.

The background to the reforms was the slowly increasing comfort of the palace. At first, the Chamber had been just that: one great draughty room, in which, as in a royal bedsit, too many conflicting functions had been crammed. In the course of the fourteenth and fifteenth centuries, however, this single room had been replaced by a suite of three more-or-less specialized apartments: the Great or Watching Chamber, the Presence Chamber and the Privy or Secret Chamber (to give them names current under the early Tudors). The Great Chamber was the guard room, where stood the Yeomen of the Guard; while the Presence Chamber was the throne room, the King's public dining-room, and a rendezvous for the court, where everyone who mattered met to gather news and to gossip. So the first two chambers were semi-public reception rooms. But the third, the Privy Chamber, was more genuinely the King's private apartment than the old, unitary Chamber had ever been. Access to it was strictly limited, while under the Tudors a complex and even more secret 'privy lodging' of bedrooms, libraries and closets was built on behind.

However, this change, though highly desirable in itself, had the effect of putting the geography of the royal palace out-of-step with the organization of the royal household, whose original foundation it had been. There were now two distinct areas 'above-stairs', but only one group of servants. The disjunction lasted until the 1490s; then Henry VII took action. The Secret or Privy Chamber was separated from

13

the other two chambers and given its own staff. At its head stood the Groom of the Stool, whose original task had been to look after the royal close-stool or commode, and to wait on the King when he relieved himself on it. To the Groom and his subordinates was transferred the entire responsibility for the King's private service; while the Lord Chamberlain's department was left with only the public ceremonial of the two outer Chambers.

These changes, which mark the division between the two-departmental household of the Middle Ages and the three-departmental household of early modern times, were big with implications for the future. But such later developments hold no clue to Henry VII's own intentions. These are suggested rather by the contrast between personnel of the old Chamber and that of the new Privy Chamber. The staff of the Chamber was large, and – in its upper ranks – distinguished: its principal servants were knights and esquires, who were drawn from the top of the gentry, at the point at which that class merged almost imperceptibly with the peerage; while the head of the department, the Lord Chamberlain, was always a peer and a councillor, and as such a figure of considerable and often major political weight. On the other hand, the staff of the Privy Chamber was small and significantly humbler, being mere gentry and sometimes hardly that. The Groom of the Stool was more substantial, but he was a courtier/ bureaucrat not a politician, who had added to his original lavatorial tasks a whole cluster of administrative functions: he was in charge of the running of the Privy Chamber and the safe-keeping of its contents; he regulated admission to the apartment; he managed an inner royal treasury known as the Privy Purse; and he acted as the King's private secretary. (Under Henry VII clear evidence is available only for the Groom's financial duties, but the rest may be reasonably inferred.)

At this stage, in short, the Groom had many responsibilities but no power. So, by substituting the Privy Chamber for the Chamber, Henry was changing from the type of personal service characteristic of the great feudal monarchies to that usual for an Italian prince. In the former, the royal service was conceived of as a more-or-less public act of homage by the King's leading subjects to the royal person, which was itself the symbol of the majesty of the kingdom; in the latter, on the other hand, the prince's body service was a purely private activity, carried out by 'persons of little worth except in the matter of knowing how to give good personal service'. The effect, and I have no doubt the intended effect, of the change was two-fold. It freed the King to work on his papers and accounts without interruption from the usual exigencies of court etiquette and routine. And it freed him from political pressure too. Not only from the great nobles, of whose power Henry was obsessively and rightly distrustful. But also from his own servants.

Here dates tell their story. The exact year in which the Privy Chamber was established is not known. But everything points to 1495. That was the climacteric year of Henry's reign, which began with the revelation that Sir William Stanley had been engaged in treasonable correspondence with Perkin Warbeck, the Yorkist pretender to the throne. Stanley was Henry's step-uncle and the man who had played the key role in the victory at Bosworth. But the blow was more than personal; it was official since Stanley was Lord Chamberlain and head of the Chamber. At the same time, the head of the Household, John, Lord Fitzwalter, the Lord Steward, was also implicated in the affair. It is hard to think that the setting up of the Privy Chamber was not a response to these events. Betrayed by both the existing departments of his household, Henry would create another. There he would retreat into comparative safety, attended on by men who were too humble to play politics.

Rarely then has any personal ruler guarded his independence more jealously or more effectively than Henry VII. An observer indeed asserted that only one man – Sir Reginald Bray – had any influence over the King, and certainly Henry kept himself so aloof from pressure that it is scarcely possible to talk of a structure of politics at all. All power was concentrated in the King's hands: that was both the strength of Henry VII's government and – in the long term – its supreme weakness.

Things were to be very different under his son. Immediately it was clear that both court and Council would recover their independence and more. But just how – in other words, what the precise structure of politics would be – took a decade to emerge from the heady, confused days of the young King's accession.

First to crystallize was the role of the King's Council. To begin with, the King's carelessness and inattention to business gave the Council as a whole much greater freedom and initiative. Then, as the results of the King's failure to act as co-ordinator of government made themselves felt more-and-more acutely, a principal minister, Thomas Wolsey, emerged who stepped into the King's place in charge of day-to-day administration. In so doing, Wolsey virtually absorbed the powers of the Council within himself.

Wolsey's position as chief councillor was fully consolidated by 1515. But at court matters remained much more fluid, despite the swift change of style brought about by Henry VIII's accession. Whereas his father had been a mere spectator of court entertainment, the son, after initial hesitation, had become an enthusiastic participant. The almost inevitable result was to turn his partners in the joust and revel into creatures that had disappeared under Henry

16

VII: court favourites of independent standing and prestige. But the structural consequences of all this were small. Only one favourite – William Compton, the Groom of the Stool – held a key office; the remainder were a rather hetero- geneous and informal group. And a short-lived one too. Some were killed in the first French war; and many of the rest were elbowed aside by Wolsey. Not in fact till significantly later, in 1518–19, with the advent of the 'minions' and the creation of the office of Gentleman of the Privy Chamber, was the place of favourite institutionalized.

Once that had happened, however, the framework of the mature structure of politics of the reign was established. The power of the court was concentrated and articulated in the hands of the Privy Chamber; while – even more acutely – the power of the Council was embodied in Wolsey. So there were now two centres of concentrated power about a King who was subject to influence and sometimes to manipulation. Inevitably, the two supplied the manipu- lators-in-chief; inevitably also the struggle for control between the two was continuous and often bitter.

But though the framework of politics was established, one further element had yet to appear: faction. Faction is the name given to the groups formed by courtiers and councillors the better to pursue their restless struggles for power and profit. These struggles were omnipresent at court, where, as Sir Francis Bryan wrote, there was always an 'overplus' of 'malice and displeasures'. No power on earth could stop such jockeying; on the other hand it was possible to prevent it escalating into the full side-taking of faction. The first recorded use of the word in the language makes this plain. This came in 1509, when Bishop Fisher praised the late Lady Margaret Beaufort in his com- memorative sermon for the vigour with which she had 'bolted', that is sifted, out 'faction or bands among [the] head officers' of her household. And in this case it was like mother, like son. Henry VII's style of management left no room for faction; Henry VIII, on the other hand, with his fluctuation, enthusiasms, and irregular handling of business, gave it an open invitation to flourish.

And it did so immediately. All the signs are there: the execution of two of Henry VIII's ministers; the formation of parties on the Council; and an unseemly row between the King's principal subject, the Duke of Buckingham, and his chief body-servant, William Compton. But it ended just as swiftly. Wolsey, as historians recognize, recreated Henry VII's style of government by putting himself as an omnicompetent minister in place of the administrator-king. It now appears that he recreated the earlier style of politics as well. Wolsey monopolized and guarded the royal favour as jealously as Henry VII had monopolized and guarded the royal power. Neither position left any place for faction. In practice of course rivals of Wolsey came on the scene from time to time. When they did, as in 1518–19, the elements of faction manifested themselves. But fleetingly. Wolsey moved ruthlessly to regain his monopoly of favour, and that done, faction was nipped in the bud.

This pattern was interrupted only in 1527 by the rise of Anne Boleyn. She broke Wolsey's monopoly of favour, which was never re-established, save momentarily and bloodily by Cromwell in 1536. The result was to unleash the forces which only Wolsey's power and personality had held in check. The Council and the Privy Chamber alike split into factions; alliances changed swiftly and bewilderingly; and the allegiance of even some leading figures was equally mutable. For vicious though the struggle could be, it still had many of the characteristics of a family quarrel. Often literally, since the governing class was so inbred that everyone had relations and friends on the other side. They could ease a transition, or protect one in a sticky corner.

But not all side-changing was mere expediency. Principle could be involved as well. Once again it all goes back to Anne Boleyn. Not only had she triggered faction; she had introduced ideology as well. Anne was a convinced evangelical and a determined patroness of the 'new' religion. She was not of course the first. But she was the first in high places to be so blatant in her preference. The effect was to polarize the court. Those who supported her tended to support 'reform' as well; while most of those who opposed her were stalwart defenders of the 'old' faith.

So policy could be just as important as personality and place in faction. Indeed it seems clear that it was the mounting dispute over religion, and the King's failure to come down firmly on either side, that screwed faction to such a pitch of intensity by the later years of Henry VIII's reign. This of course cuts clean contrary to the usual definition of faction, which sees it as being essentially personal. Two sources contribute to this view. The first is contemporary sixteenth-century usage, which was invariably pejorative: you never formed a faction; only your opponents did. While the second, which extends the first, is Edmund Burke's distinction between faction and party. A faction is a selfish and unprincipled cabal; a 'party' on the other hand, 'is a body of men united, for promoting by their joint endeavours the national interest, upon some particular principle in which they are all agreed'. To all of which F. M. Cornford's cool distinction between 'my jobs' and 'your jobs' is a sufficient reply. 'My jobs are public-spirited proposals, which happen (much to my regret) to involve the advancement of a personal friend, or (still more to my regret) of myself. Your jobs are insidious intrigues for the advancement of yourself and your friends, speciously disguised as public-spirited proposals.' The elements of personality and principle are thus common to both party and faction, as to almost all forms of political activity. They cannot serve as the basis for distinction between them. The only basis for such a distinction, in fact, is in terms of organization and structure on the one hand, and the size of the political system on the other. Factions are the relatively simple units characteristic of small-group politics; parties are the complex organs needed for large-scale or mass politics. And, though we have gained parties, we have not lost factions. Instead factions, 'wet' and 'dry', 'right' and 'left', struggle for control of the Conservative and Labour parties, and so for control of our two-party state.

And with the appearance of faction in the last years of Wolsey, the mature style of Henrician politics emerged. This was made up of two distinct but overlapping elements. First there was the minister's struggle to control the Privy Chamber, whether by purge, packing or the axe. And second there was a faction struggle which involved, principally, both the minister and the internally divided Privy Chamber. That was the case under Cromwell. After Cromwell's fall both parties became corporate and the ground was fought over by factions within both the Privy Council and the Privy Chamber. Henrician politics were not therefore a simple politics of despotism; nor on the other hand were they a conflict between ins and outs, or between court and country. Rather they were a product of faction war within the charmed circle of court and Council themselves. The modern analogy, therefore, is not the government and opposition politics of a parliamentary democracy, but the internalized feuding of a one-party state. The protagonists in this feuding – the minister and the court favourites (themselves divided by faction) – had different tasks. The minister relieved the King of the drudgery of day-to-day administration; while the favourites diverted Henry's long hours of leisure. But the distinction must not be pushed too far: to survive, the minister had to have the aptitudes of a courtier and the favourites had to have the skills of a politician and often the techniques of an administrator as well. For both, in fact, the goal they strove for was the same: influence, or, in the sixteenth century's own language, the favour of the prince.

The politics of manipulation or influence, whose outline has just been described, were peculiar and demanded particular qualities from their participants. Something of what was needed is sketched in one of the outstanding works of the age: Baldassare Castiglione's *Book of the Courtier*.

Castiglione did not start from scratch. Instead, in accordance with contemporary fashion, he based himself on a classical model – namely, the rediscovered oratorical tradition of antiquity. This was itself the product of another genre of manipulative politics: those of the Graeco-Roman city states. In their heyday these were open, face-to-face societies, without bureaucracies but ruled directly by large assemblies of citizens. Under such circumstances oratory, or the art of persuasive speech, was one of the principal keys to political success. One of the leading practitioners of the art was Cicero, and in a series of masterly dialogues he drew on his experience to delineate the qualities that made the ideal orator. Fluency of speech was only the beginning. To it he added a proficiency in every branch of learning: historical, legal, psychological, philosophical. But the orator, despite his learning, did not pursue knowledge for its own sake like the academic. For him, in contrast, knowledge was a tool of power which enabled him to master his master: the sovereign people or the Senate.

And Castiglione followed his model closely. He did so in form, for, like Cicero, his work is a series of dialogues in pursuit of the ideal; and he did so in content as well, for his

21

ideal courtier is clearly an adaptation of Cicero's ideal orator. So the courtier too must be a fine speaker who is well and widely informed. But Castiglione asks even more of him, since to the essentially intellectual qualities of the classical orator he adds the social accomplishments of the late medieval knight or gentleman. However, the purpose of this augmented universality is the same: to win favour. But whereas the orator sought the favour of many: the people or a representative assembly; the courtier pursued the favour of one: the prince. The argument is summarized at the climax of Book III by Count Fregoso, who also imbues the courtier's quest with a clear moral purpose:

the end of the perfect courtier . . . is, by means of the accomplishments attributed to him by these gentlemen, so to win for himself the mind and favour of the prince he serves that he can and always will tell him the truth about all he needs to know, without fear or risk of displeasing him.

Castiglione's work enjoyed universal success – even in remote England. Within eighteen months of its publication in 1528 Edmund Bonner, later Bishop of London, but then an up-and-coming young cleric, was begging Cromwell, as he had promised to make him a good Italian, to send him the *Book of the Courtier* in its original tongue. And Sir Thomas Wyatt certainly read it, and even felt constrained to reply to its argument in one of his greatest poems. In part, this popularity was a matter of fashion. But there was more to it than that. For Castiglione, despite all his theorizing and idealizing, reflected a reality that the early sixteenth-century English court could recognize and appreciate. Many of the leading contestants for power under Henry VIII were indeed polymaths or 'Renaissance men'; and, above all, they were orators, who laid all their talents under contribution to one end: to win the King's favour, or, more bluntly, to manipulate him.

One element is conspicuously missing from this picture: the nobility. The story of medieval politics is the story of the relationship between the King and the nobility. Manifestly the same is not true of the court-centred politics of manipulation of the reign of Henry VIII. Nobles did not fit very easily into that sort of politics at the time and recently it has been usual to ignore them entirely. One view saw them as having been broken, even wiped out, by the consistent jealousy of the first two Tudor kings; another school acknowledged the survival of noble power, but only in the localities. At the centre, it is claimed, they were content to leave the initiative to the King; happily played second fiddle to upstarts like Wolsey and Cromwell, and intervened more actively only when Henry bade them to. Maybe the heirs of Mowbray and Bohun were reduced to this. But it does not seem very likely. And Edward Stafford, Duke of Buckingham, we know, poured water over Cardinal Wolsey's shoes rather than kiss the hem of his robe. Which is not to say that the nobility always played an important role at Henry VIII's court, or that relations between the King and his peerage were consistently good. Neither assertion would be remotely true. But Henry VIII, unlike his father, deliberately adopted a noble style of life; and under him the nobility sometimes intervened decisively in court politics. And both the nobility and politics were changed as a result. By the end of the reign the peerage itself had become something different; at the beginning it was the nobility, as much as the young King, who broke the political mould of his father's reign.

2

A NEW AGE

The King and the Nobility

HENRY VIII came to the throne on 22 April 1509, aged seventeen years and ten months. It was the springtime of the year; it was also a metaphorical spring. 'This day', Thomas More wrote in a Latin poem for the coronation, 'is the end of our slavery, the fount of our liberty; the end of sadness, the beginning of joy.' Henry VIII would be a king 'to cleanse every eye of tears and substitute praise for a long moaning'. The imagery is taken from Chapter 21 of *The Book of Revelations*, which begins: 'I saw a new heaven and a new earth.' Now of course every new reign is hailed as a new age (even 1952 produced the 'new Elizabethans'). But 1509 was different – as More's poem shows. It is not a mere paean of praise for Henry VIII; it is also a political programme for a point-by-point reversal of the political and fiscal policies of the government of Henry VII. No longer, More said, would the nobility be oppressed, or the merchant deterred by taxes; people could once again show their possessions without fear of having them stolen by the government, and informers could be ignored. So black, in fact, is the picture of the dead King that years later, when the poem was published, a French critic, Germanus Brixius, accused More of disloyalty to the Crown. At the time, however, he was sufficiently sure of his ground to give the poem to Henry VIII in a handsome

24

presentation copy, decorated with red and white roses.

But this new age, hailed by More and blessed by Henry VIII, was not a stepping forward into the Brave New World of the Renaissance. Instead, it was right-about-turn to the Middle Ages. More's political programme was reactionary, and its most important item was the first: the freeing of the nobility from oppression. The medieval nobility were the oldest element in politics. They were the greatest landowners, and that alone, when land was power, made them politically supreme. In addition might had been turned into right by a series of constitutional edicts. These, of which Magna Carta was the most famous, confirmed their privileges as individuals and acknowledged their collective right to participate in the government of the kingdom. The order reached its apogee in the fifteenth century. By then it had completed its evolution into a very small hereditary caste which rarely numbered more than sixty and often far fewer. The members of the nobility were distinguished from each other by a strict hierarchy of titles from duke, marquess and earl at the top, to viscount and baron at the bottom. And they were cut off from everybody else, however rich or ancient their lineage, by their right, which descended to their heirs, to a seat in the Upper House of Parliament. At the same time the restraining hand of the King was weak. The nobility flourished in both the wars of Henry V and in the long minority of his son, Henry VI. After that even a strong King would have had problems; as it was, Henry VI's combination of feckless-ness and favouritism bred first instability and then the open struggle of the Wars of the Roses. The Wars, which were really a series of short, sharp engagements rather than the all-embracing conflagration of Shakespeare's imagination, saw the most flamboyant assertions of noble power, as an Earl of Warwick or a Duke of Buckingham made and unmade kings.

But there was also a contrary movement. In the first series of battles, from 1459 to 1461, the great majority of the nobility was involved; at Bosworth, however, only six peers fought for Richard III and a mere two for Henry Tudor, and they were both penniless exiles. The nobility, in short, had opted for neutrality. Many of the politically ambitious and active nobles had been killed, and the losses of those in whose veins the blood royal flowed were particularly heavy. The rest were cowed, like Lord Mountjoy, who in his will written within three weeks of Bosworth advised his sons 'never to take the state of baron on them . . ., nor to desire to be great about princes, for it is dangerous'. But not only was the nobility weaker; the King was stronger. The royal lands were greater in extent than they had been for hundreds of years; while the King's own following of knights and gentlemen was uniquely large and powerful. They had become the dominant political force in the crucial south-east, and they had infiltrated the administration to make government the King's government in deed as well as in name.

Henry VII pressed home this advantage ruthlessly. The penalty for being on the losing side in battle against the King was treason. This involved death and forfeiture of property by a procedure called attainder. Previous kings, often desperate for support, had reversed attainders pretty freely. Not so Henry. Nor did he fill the resulting gaps in the peerage with new creations. But his particular severity was reserved for nobles of the immediate Yorkist line: the Earl of Warwick, son of Edward IV's brother the Duke of Clarence, was imprisoned and eventually executed; the de la Poles, offspring of Edward's sister, were first demoted from duke to earl and then driven into exile and rebellion; while the heirs of the Greys, Marquesses of Dorset, and the Courtenays, Earls of Devon, the first descended from Edward IV's stepson and the second married to his daughter Catherine, had their titles and lands frozen and their persons imprisoned. Young Grey, transferred to Calais in 1507, would even, it was rumoured, have been 'put to death, if [Henry] had lived longer'. The fate of the rest was less dramatically unpleasant. They were not imprisoned; instead they were bound with chains of gold. The instrument was the bond. A bond is an agreement with a penalty clause for non-performance. By the end of the reign some two thirds of the nobility had been required to enter into such agreements with the King. Some were to guarantee the payment of a debt to the King; some were to ensure the proper performance of an office. But many were dangerously open-ended. The condition was good behaviour, and the interpreter of good behaviour was the King. These bonds were imposed and assessed by a sub-committee, or 'by-court', of the Council called the Council-learned-at-law, whose dominant members were Sir Richard Empson and Edmund Dudley.

For the nobility as a whole, then, Henry VII's death came as a profound relief. And they made their feelings about the old King plain by their praise of the new. 'Heaven and earth rejoice; everything is full of milk and honey and nectar', wrote William, Lord Mountjoy, who had conspicuously ignored his father's advice to keep out of politics. 'Avarice has fled the country', he continued, 'our King is not after gold, or gems, or precious metals, but virtue, glory, immortality.' Others did more than write letters. Henry VIII had been with his father when he died at his favourite palace of Richmond on 21 April. Next day he came to London and took up his quarters in the Tower. There he remained, the Marquess of Winchester recalled long afterwards, until the Duke of Buckingham and the Earl of Oxford, the senior peers by rank and by office and experience respectively, came to court. Then the Council assembled to debate the all-important question of how the impressionable young King should be brought up (he was, after all, barely of age): should he 'be brought up in worldly knowledge, or else in pleasure and liberty, leaving the care to his Council'. The resolution was 'to bring him up in all pleasure, for otherwise he should grow too hard among his subjects as the King his father did'.

These are an old man's memories. But the gist is probably right. With the death of the King the authority of his ordinary councillors lapsed. Into the gap stepped the nobility as the King's councillors by birth. They used their position to launch an immediate attack on both the personnel and the policies of the old regime. Empson and Dudley, the two councillors most closely identified with the oppression of their order, were arrested. Then, as London filled with peers for first the King's wedding to Catherine of Aragon and then the coronation, the Great Council was summoned. The Great Council was an assembly of all the peers, and so really a Parliament without the Commons. The assembly met in June; the following month a series of high-powered investigatory commissions, known as commissions of 'oyer and terminer', were issued for the whole kingdom. Not only were the commissioners to examine every crime from treason to trespass; they were also to hear complaints about infringements 'of the statute of Magna Carta concerning the liberties of England', as well as any other breaches of 'the laws and customs of our kingdom of England'.

The government in short was inviting criticisms of its own past executive actions. It is rare today; it was totally extraordinary in the sixteenth century. The last time anything like it had happened was in the dark days of Henry VI. Then, in 1450, another meeting of the Great Council had advised the sending out of a general commission of 'oyer and terminer'. But that was in response to the rising of the Commons in Cade's rebellion and their complaint of misgovernment in Kent. Now it was the Lords themselves who were complaining of the misgovernment of England and citing Magna Carta to prove it. In this they were following in the footsteps of their ancestors, who had harked back to the Great Charter whenever relations between Crown and nobility reached a crisis point, as in 1258–9 under Henry III, or in 1311 under Edward II. In the troubles of the fifteenth century Magna Carta slept, for the problems arose from the weakness and not the strength of the monarchy. But with the revival of the King's power, the traditional symbol of resistance to royal tyranny became relevant once more.

After such tremendous preliminaries, what was actually done was almost bound to seem small beer. Empson and Dudley were condemned and eventually executed; and several bonds were cancelled on the grounds that they were 'made by undue means of certain of the Learned Council of our . . . late father . . . contrary to law, reason and good conscience, to the manifest charge and peril of the soul of our . . . late father'. But the investigatory commissions were wound up in November, since, it was claimed, the worst cases had been dealt with. The action then shifts to Parliament itself, which met in January 1510. The great nobles were prominent in the opening ceremonies: Buckingham carried the cap of estate; his son Henry bore the sword; while the Earl of Oxford as Great Chamberlain and the Earl of Surrey as Lord Treasurer stood on the King's left as the Lord Chancellor read his speech. The latter was more than the usual tissue of platitudes. Henry VII had called only one Parliament in the last ten years of his reign; the Chancellor now pointedly held forth on the advantages of frequent Parliaments, which gave subjects an opportunity to air grievances and seek redress. This was a clear signal that the repudiation of the old regime was to continue and it did. Some of the legal loopholes through which the Council-learned had driven their nasty engines were blocked up; more importantly, the whole basis in law of Henry VII's privatization of national finance into his Chamber was called into question.

Finally came the most stunning reversal of all. There was, it is assumed, a 'Tudor dynastic policy', in which Henry VII and Henry VIII pursued to the death every branch and twiglet of the rival house of York. This, as we have seen, holds good for Henry VII. But once again Henry VIII stood his father's policies on their head. Not only were the peripheral Greys and Courtenays restored; so too was the direct Yorkist line when Margaret, daughter of the Duke of Clarence, was made Countess of Salisbury, and her son created Lord Montague.

Clearly the nobility knew what they were doing in all this. But did the King? Here it is worth going back to the last time an adult Prince of Wales had followed his father on the throne. This was in 1413 when Henry V had succeeded Henry IV. Henry V too had identified with noble opposition to his father – and even before his death. The reason was war. Henry V's life and kingship were devoted to a renewal of the Hundred Years War against France. And that could be done successfully only with the whole-hearted backing of the nobility and their vast retinues. Harry the Eighth set himself the same warlike ambition as Harry the Fifth. And it had to be pursued by the same means of an alliance with the nobility. Henry VIII's army, at the end of his reign as well as at the beginning, was not a royal army. Instead it was an 'army royal': that is, a loose confederation, under the King himself as war lord, of the royal household and its retinues, and the great lords and their retinues.

But there was a difference. Henry V made his kingship a religion. Warrior though he was, he handled his finances (and every aspect of his government) with the same meticulous attention to detail as Henry VII. Not so Henry VIII. The Lords, Winchester tells us, resolved to bring the young King up 'in all pleasure'. Henry VIII himself proclaimed:

Pastime with good company
I love and shall until I die

Hunt, sing, and dance
My heart is set
All goodly sport
To my comfort
Who shall me let?

Who should prevent ('let') him indeed? Not the nobility. Not only had they agreed that 'pastime' would stop him growing 'too hard upon his subjects as the King his father did'; the nobility also supplied his chief companions in his pleasures. Among Henry VIII's first intimate circle of fellow jousters and revellers were the Earl of Wiltshire, Buckingham's younger brother, Sir Edward Howard, Surrey's second son, Sir Thomas Knyvet, who had married Surrey's eldest daughter, and Sir Thomas Boleyn, who had married the Earl's second daughter. Thomas Grey, now restored to the Marquess of Dorset, joined the circle in 1511, while nearly all its remaining members – such as Henry Bourchier, Earl of Essex, and Sir Edward Neville, younger brother of George, Lord Abergavenny – were similarly patrician. The only exceptions were Charles Brandon and Sir Henry Guildford, whose origins lay within the Tudor's own knightly following, and William Compton, who came from nowhere.

In this 'good company' Henry made his court resemble the marvellous marginal illustrations in the later medieval psalter: now it was hunting and hawking; now jousting, or running at the ring, or fighting at the barriers; now revels by torchlight. Influence and manipulation hardly entered into it. Henry, who had come to the throne on the eve of St George's Day, saint of knights and nobles as well as patron saint of England, thought, felt and acted like a noble. While the nobility, for their part, rejoiced to have a king who was one of themselves. At the same time, however, such a change in the style of kingship did have major political repercussions. The nobility who had been 'out' were now 'in'; while the 'ruling élite' of Henry VII were in the wilderness. They had seen their governmental methods repudiated and two of their number executed; while the nobility now occupied the commanding heights of Tudor politics in the Council and the court. But though the old guard were out they were not out for the count. With their administrative experience, in which the nobility were singularly lacking, they had retained an important place on the Council; they also, rather surprisingly, remained in command of the Order of the Garter. And from these positions they mounted a reasonably effective rearguard action.

Everything turned on the King's attitude to war: the mock war of the joust as well as the real thing. Nature had built Henry to be a jouster. He had height, bull-like strength, horsemanship and agility. Of course, since he was a king, his prowess was exaggerated. But it was not imaginary. Jousting is not all-in wrestling. No doubt the odd tournament could have been fixed, but not Henry's lengthy series of victories against the best knights at his court. He had shown his aptitude early. In 1508 he had spent day after day tilting at Richmond and in 1507, when he was still only fifteen, he had been like a boy at his first big football match, eager to talk with the jousters and encouraging, though a prince,

Gentlemen of low degree
In his presence
To speak of arms and other defence

But always his father's restraining hand was there. With the death of Henry VII's elder son Arthur in 1502, the whole Tudor dynasty hung by the single thread of Prince Henry's life. Friendly bouts with chosen companions were acceptable, but the risks of participating in full-scale public jousting were not.

The frustration of a born sportsman and performer forbidden to show off his talents in the proper arena must have been immense. This makes his caution on coming to the throne all the more remarkable. For instead of kicking over the traces immediately, Henry waited for a full nine months before jousting publicly. Even then he was hardly brazen about it. Instead he rode incognito, 'unknown to all persons and unlooked for', with just one companion, his most confidential servant, William Compton. And it was only when Compton 'was . . . hurt sore and likely to die', that the disguise was broken by someone in the know crying 'God save the King' in alarm. Next month, in February 1510, Henry also joined in the revel for the first time. The taboo on participation now broken, he of course became unstoppable. But still, as the chroniclers repeatedly tell us, there were worried murmurs amid the applause, 'insomuch that it was plainly spoken, that steel was not so strong, but it might be broken, nor no horse could be so sure of foot, but he may fall'. These 'doubters' were 'the ancient fathers' – almost certainly the surviving councillors of Henry VII, who were repeating in public what hitherto they had urged in private.

Their advice then had kept the King from jousting for several months; it probably kept him out of real war even longer. From the beginning, Henry had been spoiling for a

33

fight with France. Even his precipitate marriage to Catherine of Aragon can be seen in this light. The longer Catherine had been kept in England after the death of Prince Arthur, her first husband, the less likely her remarriage to Henry had seemed. Yet within days of the accession Henry had announced his determination to marry her, which he had done on 11 June. Why? He wanted a wife certainly; he might even have wanted Catherine of Aragon. But most of all he wanted the support of Catherine's father, Ferdinand of Aragon, his obvious ally in a war with France. More direct signs of hostility to France were given as well. In the first weeks of the reign Henry had rudely walked out of an audience with the French Ambassador, and in the summer of 1509, when he learned that a conciliatory letter had been sent in his name to Louis XII, he exploded in public rage: 'Who wrote this letter? I ask peace of the King of France, who dare not look at me, let alone make war?' But for all Henry's bombast, the proffered peace treaty was signed in March 1510. Two months later, however, another treaty was concluded with Ferdinand which effectively nullified the one with France. These contradictory policies might have been the effect of over-subtle diplomacy. Much more likely, they were the consequences, as the Spanish Ambassador thought, of party division within the Council. One group, consisting mainly of Henry VII's old councillors, stuck to a French alliance and the pacific policies of the previous reign; the other, made up largely of the high nobility, wanted war with France and an offensive alliance with Ferdinand's Spanish kingdoms.

With Henry's support and leadership the war party was bound to win. But it took a long time. When the Great Council was reconvened in 1511, the anti-war party at first carried the day. Only Henry's own pleadings and some opportune revelations of French perfidy got agreement

1. Henry VII and Henry VIII.
Holbein's working drawing for part of his life-size mural of the Tudor
dynasty. The inscription hailed Henry VII for restoring domestic peace
and Henry VIII for establishing true religion.

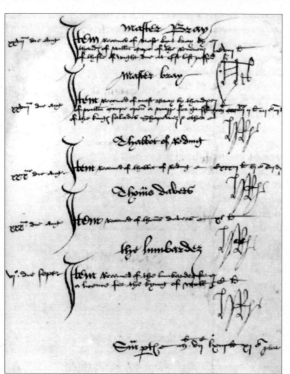

2. Henry VII teaches himself the business of government. A page from his receipt book of August 1492, showing his monogram change from the soldier's fist that he had used hitherto (at the top) to the clerk's hand that he employed henceforth.

3. Pietro Torrigiano's painted terracotta bust of Henry VII suggests the imperious public face of the 'kingship of distance'.

. Unlike his father, Henry VIII maintained a grand style is his private life. Here he dines in his Privy Chamber, alone and served on bended knee. At the back, councillors and courtiers; at the front, Ushers with staffs of office, and a buffet plate to one side.

5. Baldassare Castiglione, painted by his friend Raphael. His *Book of the Courtier*, printed in 1528, was the most influential guide to political and social behaviour throughout Europe.

6. Holbein's drawing of Sir Thomas Wyatt: courtier, ambassador and rejected lover of Anne Boleyn. His poetry is a brilliantly idiosyncratic guide to the delights and dangers of the court.

7. Sir Thomas More, painted by his house guest Holbein in 1527 in the gold livery chain of a King's servant. He began by welcoming Henry VIII as a liberator, but ended by defying him to the death over the break with Rome.

8. A self-portrait of Hans Holbein, who spent most of his mature years in Englan His great portfolio of portrait drawings, now i the Royal Collection, is the most vivid record of a Renaissance court.

9. Henry VIII, going to open the Parliament of 1512 and surrounded by the lords who dominated his first years: Buckingham with the cap of maintenance in front, the Earl of Oxford with the staff of the Lord Great Chamberlain behind and the Earl of Surrey far right.

10. Holbein's drawing of Sir Henry Guildford, Controller of the Household, and Master of the Revels. As such he was responsible for devising the subjects and settings of both jousts and masques.

11. Cardinal Wolsey by an unknown artist. None of his surviving portraits takes us very far into the character of Henry's extraordinary chief councillor.

12. Holbein's drawing of William Warham, Archbishop of Canterbury, in extreme old age. Warham resigned the Chancellorship to Wolsey but by outliving him denied him the archbishopric of Canterbury.

13. Thomas Howard, who succeeded his father as Duke of Norfolk in 1524. Lord Treasurer and Earl Marshal, hence the white staff and the baton, he was the leader of religious and political conservatism.

14. Richard Fox, Bishop of Winchester, when old and blind. Earlier he had been the most forceful survivor of the old guard of Henry VII's reign and had promoted Wolsey to out-flank the noble war party.

15. Lady Margaret Beaufort, Henry VIII's grandmother, at prayer. She set a model for the rigid disciplining of her household, which her more easy-going grandson did not attempt to follow.

16. Hampton Court from the river. To the left is Wolsey's original palace; to the right the vast range of royal apartments added by Henry VIII and rebuilt by Wren in the seventeenth century, and centre the Privy Garden with its posts and railed flower beds.

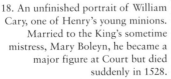

17. An engraving of Sir Nicholas Carew, the Master of the Horse. Beginning as a star jouster, he matured into a conservative politician; helped destroy Anne Boleyn and was himself executed in 1539.

18. An unfinished portrait of William Cary, one of Henry's young minions. Married to the King's sometime mistress, Mary Boleyn, he became a major figure at Court but died suddenly in 1528.

even to a limited intervention as Ferdinand's ally. The intervention was a dismal failure. Nevertheless, even though national honour was now at stake, in the Great Council of 1512 it took all the King's fiery eloquence to carry the case for a full-scale attack on France by an army royal commanded by Henry himself. The nobility had won. War it was. France was invaded and the town of Thérouanne invested. A French relief column badly underestimated the odds against it and fled; so precipitately indeed that the engagement was called the Battle of the Spurs by the English, who magnified the incident into a notable victory. Thérouanne then fell and was razed to the ground. Warned by its fate, the nearby city of Tournai surrendered. This was kept and was garrisoned and refortified at vast expense. It was to be a second Calais: part symbol of England's claim to France, part bridgehead for future invasions. All this was a mere side-show for France, whose main armies were engaged in Italy. Meanwhile England had a side-show of her own since the Scots, ever eager to make trouble in England's backyard, invaded. The invaders were met by the Earl of Surrey at Flodden. There they suffered a catastrophic defeat in which the King, James IV, and most of the nobility were killed.

Now indeed was a time of victories – and spoils. These Henry distributed with a lavish hand. On 1 February 1514 both Surrey, the victor of Flodden, and Charles Brandon, the King's favourite jousting companion who had distinguished himself at Tournai, were made dukes. Brandon was given the dukedom of Suffolk, forfeited by the de la Poles; while Surrey at last recovered the family dukedom of Norfolk, which his father had lost by his support for Richard III. As well, to commemorate Surrey's 'generalship, guidance and governance' at Flodden, the royal arms of Scotland were added to his own, with the lion pierced through the mouth with an arrow, as the body of James IV had been. On the same day Sir Charles Somerset, a Beaufort bastard and commander at Tournai, was made Earl of Worcester; while three months later Sir Edward Stanley, the younger son of the Earl of Derby who had commanded the left wing at Flodden, was created Lord Mounteagle: 'because he won the hill or *mount* against the Scots . . . and [because] his ancestors bare in their crest the *eagle*.'

The good old days were back with a vengeance: not for half a century had there been such a crop of creations. The nobility had got all it wanted from war: profit, prestige and power. But there was a price to be paid. There had been casualties in the war, of which the most notable were two of the closest of Henry's first group of favourites, the brothers-in-law Sir Thomas Knyvet and Sir Edward Howard. And war needed not only commanders, but organizers. It threw up one of genius, Thomas Wolsey. The deaths of Knyvet and Howard opened the way for a new generation at court, while the rise of Wolsey offered a much more immediate challenge to the nobility's dominance of the Council.

3

THE CARDINAL

IN HIS PORTRAIT Thomas Wolsey, Lord Chancellor of England and Cardinal-Archbishop of York, looks like a man who had always had it good. He must have been fifty when it was painted, and it was an age when men aged fast. Even so his face is smooth and unwrinkled. The jowls and neck are heavy and bull-like. But the rest of the features are delicate to the point of effeminacy. The lips are full, red and slightly pursed; while the eyebrows are raised in quizzical interrogation. Something was not just so. But whatever he was dissatisfied with, it was not himself.

His youthfulness was not the result of a quiet life, however. Perhaps instead energy and excitement were the preservatives. He drove himself as hard as he drove others; and his career was a giddy switchback from success to failure. He was born in 1472 or 1473 in Ipswich, Suffolk, where his father was a butcher and innkeeper. He never forgot his origins, and never forgave others for remembering them too. Somehow he was sent to Magdalen College, Oxford, and, young though he was, outshone all his contemporaries. He was 'the boy bachelor' by fifteen, and subsequently became Fellow and Bursar of his college, as well as Master of Magdalen School. Ordination came automatically with his fellowship; it was not a question of vocation and he never behaved as though it was. But though his priesthood sat lightly on him, he took his churchmanship very seriously.

So far so good. His origins were humbler than most, and his undergraduate career more meteoric. Otherwise it was a beginning typical of many an ambitious cleric who was to rise high in the royal service. But then something went wrong. The next rung on the ladder to promotion was a doctorate, usually in canon law. This Wolsey never took; indeed, he fairly soon left Oxford under some sort of cloud. Thereafter he was tutor or chaplain in a variety of socially distinguished but politically unimportant households. Wolsey's final appointment of this type was to the Deputy, that is Governor, of England's dependency of Calais. The Deputy died in 1507, having first recommended Wolsey to Henry VII, who made him his chaplain. Despite legend, however, he made no immediate impact at court. In short, up to 1509 Wolsey's career was sterile and directionless. The boy bachelor had become a burnt-out case in his late thirties.

Why had so much promise achieved so little? Bad luck was partly to blame. One patron, Henry Dean, died only two years after being made Archbishop of Canterbury; while another, the Marquess of Dorset, fell into acute political disfavour. But the real problem probably lay in Wolsey himself. Two stories about his early years are suggestive. He seems to have got the push from Oxford for lavishing Magdalen's money on building works without proper authorization; while shortly afterwards he was put in the stocks at his parish of Limington, Dorset, 'tradition has it', for offending the local bigwig by his 'exuberant behaviour after a fair'. So already much of the man was there. Already there was a tendency to act first and seek authority afterwards; an insatiable love of grand building; a brusqueness with his betters; and a flamboyance and self-indulgence, which can also be seen as a huge capacity for enjoyment. His most important trait, the sheer, over-whelming force of his personality, needed a larger field of action fully to appear. But it can be safely inferred. Wolsey, in short, was brilliant but he was not safe. And the reign of Henry VII was an age for safe men.

What turned him from an ageing and disappointed might-have-been into a too great success was the accession of Henry VIII. Henry, for all his faults, was a big man, mentally as well as physically. And he liked to surround himself with others who were similarly proportioned. Some of his courtiers and favourites were of the same massive build, like Sir Henry Guildford, or Sir Edward Neville, who was tall and broad enough to be mistaken for the King himself when both were disguised in a masque. Henry also liked magnanimity or greatness of mind. It was absence of this, just as much as its lack of magnificence, that had alienated him from his father's regime and driven a wedge between him and his father's councillors. Not that the latter were little men. But they were consistently successful careerists, who had jumped the right hoops at the right time. Such a process does not necessarily eliminate talent, and William Warham, the Archbishop of Canter-bury, had weight and Richard Fox, Bishop of Winchester, even had flair. The rest, however, blended impressive abilities with slight dullness.

It was to find something more congenial that Henry had turned to the nobility. He had mixed success. Several of the nobles, or at least their sons and younger brothers, were capable of keeping up with the King in the tiltyard and the hunt. Their intellectual capacities were another matter. In theory, magnanimity was the key aristocratic virtue; in practice it was hard to legislate for a state of mind and only a handful of nobility showed much sign of possessing it. Three in particular stood out: Edward Stafford, Duke of Buckingham, and the Howards, father and son and both

called Thomas, who became respectively Duke of Norfolk
and Earl of Surrey in 1514. Stafford and the Howards were
the same in their consuming ambition but differed in
everything else. Buckingham was inordinately proud: of his
ancient lineage, his vast wealth, his royal blood. His pride
made him half-reluctant to bow the knee to the King
himself and utterly unwilling to concede anything to
anyone else. This stiff-neckedness quickly disqualified him
from playing a serious part in the subtle politics of the
court and he more-and-more withdrew. The Howards
were made of a more malleable metal. They had first won
their dukedom by devoted service to Richard III; they had
regained it by serving the Tudors just as well. And events
were to show that there was nothing, not even their own
children, that they would refuse to sacrifice on the altar of
royal favour. This made them always a formidable force in
politics; but always too the supremacy that they longed for
eluded them. They had great name and reputation, and
great military skills; they lacked only greatness itself.

So in Henry VIII England had a king who aspired to
greatness. The councillors he inherited failed to share the
vision; those he had chosen glimpsed it but were incapable
of realizing it. Into the vacuum stepped Wolsey, who must
have stood out as much as if he had already been wearing
cardinalic red. He was promoted, it seems, by Fox. The
latter, having quality himself, was capable of recognizing it
in others, and got Wolsey made royal Almoner and
councillor towards the end of 1509. The Almoner was a
member of the Chapel Royal, and his formal responsibility
was the distribution of the doles of food and of money to
the poor who thronged the King's gate. More importantly,
he was also one of the small group of low-ranking
councillors who held the fort at court during the frequent
absence of the great men of the realm. In this capacity
Wolsey wrote his first surviving letter to Fox from Windsor

in September 1511. The letter shows his characteristic warmth, impetuousness and partisanship. He denounces the latest successes of the war party. Henry had lent Lord Darcy £1000 to get his expeditionary force to back Ferdinand of Aragon off the ground. The venture had ended in fiasco; nevertheless Henry had just been persuaded to convert the loan into an outright gift. 'Thus the King's money goeth away in every corner.' On the other hand, Surrey, the leader of the war party, had had such a frosty reception when he came to court that he went home next day and had not subsequently returned. Eagerly Wolsey suggested that his absence be made permanent by depriving him of his lodgings at court. But though Surrey's departure from court would do much, Fox's coming would do more. Surrey's son, and Henry's great favourite, Sir Edward Howard, had fought an engagement off the Downs in August 1511 in which he had killed a Scottish sea captain and captured two of his ships. Now Howard was urging Henry on against the Scots, 'by whose wanton means', Wolsey continues, 'his grace spendeth much money, and is more disposed to war than peace. Your presence shall be very necessary to suppress this appetite.'

All good stuff and music to Fox's ears. But within a year Wolsey had reversed his position on all fronts. The partisan of peace was being denounced as 'the author of war'; and the loyal dependant of Fox had become the ally of the Howards. Why? Two things had happened. Fox and the old councillors had finally lost their battle for control of the government. This must have happened by the spring of 1512, for in May well-informed rumours were circulating in Normandy of an imminent English invasion. French victories in Italy and wariness of the Scots were causing last-minute delays, 'but the young councillors, by whom the King is ruled, advise this invasion'. Even more important was the reason for the victory of the war party.

It had won ultimately because the King had wanted it to win. In 1511 Wolsey was still thinking of 'suppressing' the royal 'appetite for war'; within months he must have known that this was useless. But if the appetite could not be suppressed, Wolsey would exploit it and for his own ends.

Every writer on Wolsey has tried to glean support for his interpretation of the Cardinal from the thin evidence of these early years. J. J. Scarisbrick saw Wolsey already committed to peace even if forced to wage war; A. F. Pollard, on the other hand, detected the loyal servant of Rome. Wolsey's first biographer and sometime gentleman usher, George Cavendish, is no exception, but he looked not to policy but to technique. Wolsey rose, he claimed, because 'he was the most earnest and readiest among all the council to advance the King's only will and pleasure without any respect to the case'.

This would seem to make the King the mainspring of policy and that indeed is what some current scholarship is claiming. Such a view is too simple, however. Henry obviously wanted to joust and to wage war from the moment he came to the throne. Yet it took him nine months to appear in the lists and nearly three years to lead his troops in battle. Meanwhile, he hesitated and wavered as conflicting advice and pressures pushed him this way and that. When it was exerted, the royal will could not be gainsaid. But Henry screwed up his resolution only slowly, and there were many slips betwixt cup and lip. All this made relations between the King and his courtiers and councillors much more complex than command on the one side and obedience on the other. Things were muddied further by the realities of government. Even when the King had a clear policy, he was sometimes sketchy about details and often frankly indifferent about means, particularly financial means. Executing policy; paying for it; even choosing its agents, were tasks for his ministers, not the King. In short, in carrying out policy, a minister enjoyed almost total discretion; and if he played his cards right, he could formulate much of its substance as well.

For councillors trained under Henry VII, who had not only made policy but overseen its execution in detail too, such a royal style was bewildering and deplorable. Naturally they tried to remould the son in the image of his father, and persuaded 'the King to have some time an intercourse into the Council, there to hear what was done in weighty matters'. Equally naturally Henry VIII hated these well-intended lessons. For Wolsey, on the other hand, the King's indifference to business was a heaven-sent opportunity. Instead of deflecting him from his pleasures, he encouraged him. Henry's noble councillors, of course, had done the same. The difference was that Wolsey was far better at the execution of policy and infinitely better in his handling of the King. Henry wanted to be great and Wolsey seemed the man who could put greatness in his grasp.

Professor Elton is sceptical. Wolsey, he writes, was lucky to be included in a series called 'Twelve English Statesmen' 'even as twelfth man'. Maybe. But Wolsey is one of the most famous statesmen in English history – second only perhaps to Churchill, who resembled him in not a few ways. Being famous for five minutes is one thing; being famous for 450 years quite another. Some people are great because they transcend their own times. That I think would be Professor Elton's view. Wolsey belongs to the latter group. The early sixteenth century was an age of rhetoric. Henry's boyish enthusiasm for 'virtue, glory, immortality' was fed and flattered by humanist rhetoricians who should have known better. But they paid the price, for they were only acting as John the Baptist to the coming master orator: Thomas Wolsey.

Once again, Cavendish grasps the point and presents Wolsey above all as the courtier-orator. He had, he says, 'a filed tongue and ornate eloquence', which sounds like the kind of style that would appeal to Henry's taste, if that is the right word, for the lush and lavish. In fact, the extravagance of Wolsey's spoken style was so characteristic that it could be parodied at the end of the sixteenth century in *The Chronicle* found among the papers of George Wyatt (grandson of the poet Sir Thomas); while we can still see the written style in the process of composition in Wolsey's autograph corrections to a draft of the Eltham Ordinances of 1526. His pen scarcely touches points of substance; rather, sonorous adjectives and echoing repetition are its aims. But all this is really beside the point, since nothing is more foreign to one age than the rhetorical fashion of another: if Gladstone sounds odd, and he does, what may not be allowed to Wolsey?

Persuasive speech was the crown of the art of the courtier-orator, but it was not its all. For also, as we have seen, both Cicero and Castiglione insisted that their ideals needed to be men of universal talents. And intellectually at least Wolsey came near to the blue-print. He was an administrator of genius, an amateur lawyer of energy and originality, a diplomat of distinction, and a discerning, as well as lavish, patron of music, scholarship and the visual arts. But these attributes were not ends in themselves; they served only as auxiliaries to language in the task of influencing the King.

Influence means two things. First was the direct manipulation of the royal mind. Here Wolsey's genuine connoisseurship was laid under heavy contribution:

Every time he wished to obtain something from Henry, he introduced the matter casually into his conversation; then he brought out some small present

44

or another, a beautifully fashioned dish, for example, or a jewel or ring or gifts of that sort, and while the King was admiring the gift intently, Wolsey would adroitly bring forward the project on which his mind was fixed.

The writer is Polydore Vergil, the Italian author of the best contemporary history of England. He hated Wolsey, and recently it has been fashionable to disregard him. I cannot see in principle why a man's friends are more likely to tell the truth about him than his enemies. And in any case the historian is not allowed the luxury of choosing his witnesses. He has to make do with what he has got. Nor in this instance does it really matter. Polydore Vergil the enemy offers the same judgement as George Cavendish the friend and loyal servant, but with the added edge that it is a judgement of one professional humanist on another.

But influence was something much broader than this face-to-face handling of the King. Indeed it affected the whole presentation of policy. Wolsey was perhaps the most effective packager of policy before our own age of public relations, which is only rhetoric disguised as pseudo social science. Grandeur and grandiloquence were the key. Wolsey was not content to sign a treaty with France, particularly when it involved the humiliating surrender of Tournai, the fruit of his and his King's 'great' victory in the first French war. Instead there had to be a grand treaty of Universal Peace. Nor subsequently could Wolsey simply negotiate between Charles V and Francis I, frankly offering England's alliance to the highest bidder. That was sordid; instead he, the butcher's son, would arbitrate the differences of the two greatest sovereigns in Europe. He could not even put a foot in the street without turning it into a procession.

By means such as these Wolsey rose faster than any other

subject in Henry's reign, becoming Bishop of Lincoln and Tournai and Archbishop of York in 1514, and Cardinal and Lord Chancellor in 1515. He also retained the royal favour longer. He remained in unchallenged power for more than fifteen years and even after his fall kept such a hold on the King that his enemies had to bend all their energies to keeping the Cardinal well away from the court,

> *lest his nigh-being to the King, [the latter] might at length some one time resort to him and so call him home again, considering the great affection and love that the King daily show[ed] towards him.*

So oratory helped Wolsey win power, keep in favour, and present policy. It even contributed to the substance of policy as well. His rhetorical intelligence meant that he tended to see policies not as ends in themselves, but rather as stage-props in the game of manipulation. They were a rhetoric that was intended to change, not the state of Tudor England, but the state of Henry Tudor's mind. So it is pointless to complain that his reforms, because they were never finished, did not endure; Wolsey himself – thanks largely to the changes of front marked by these bursts of reform – endured one and a half decades in supreme power and that was enough. For Wolsey, as for that modern rhetorical politician, Harold Wilson, power was not only something to be used, it was also – with all its trappings – to be enjoyed.

But all this lay in the future. What mattered in these early years was the speed with which Wolsey monopolized power. 'Who', Cavendish asked rhetorically, 'was now high in favour but Master Almoner? Who hath all the suit but Master Almoner? And who ruled all under the King but Master Almoner?' It was as though, once whetted, Wolsey's appetite became insatiable. He could not be satisfied with a part or even a major share in the royal counsels; nothing less than the entirety of power would do. Some of the possible obstacles, like Sir Edward Howard or Sir Thomas Knyvet, were among the fallen of the first French war; others may have removed themselves voluntarily. Fox and Warham, the two most distinguished survivors of Henry VII's Council, were already old, and Fox was going blind. Both were men of genuine religiosity who had neglected their dioceses to serve the King. Now perhaps they decided to serve God instead. Warham resigned as Chancellor in 1515 and withdrew to Canterbury; Fox surrendered the Privy Seal the following year and devoted his formidable energies to his bishopric and to rebuilding the choir of Winchester cathedral.

On the other hand, Charles Brandon, who had been created Duke of Suffolk in 1514, had the most self-interested reasons for coming to terms with Wolsey. Mary, Henry VIII's vivacious younger sister, had been married to Louis XII of France as a pledge of peace in 1514. She had protested vigorously, and had been delighted when death had freed her from her elderly husband on 1 January 1515. But just to make sure that she was not used as a dynastic pawn a second time she secretly married Brandon, who had been sent to escort her back to England. Henry had been consulted about the possibility of the match and had been sympathetic. But the haste and secrecy of the actual wedding put the couple beyond the pale. In these circumstances Brandon was only too willing to take up Wolsey's offer to mediate and put himself more-or-less unreservedly in his hands.

But for the rest – Buckingham, Surrey, Norfolk – the juggernaut of Wolsey's power simply rolled over them. The result was a different sort of politics. In the first years of the reign power had been held by a Council meeting at court. The Council was divided into two factions, who bid against one another for the royal favour. This dragged Henry willy-nilly (mostly it was nilly) into the actual processes of government, and quite often he must have been the real arbiter of policy. Wolsey's rise changed all this. Royal favour was no longer divided but concentrated in the Cardinal. So faction vanished, or at least went underground. And as it did so, the centre of politics swung away from the King's court to Wolsey's court.

'Why come ye not to court?' cheekily asked John Skelton, the Poet Laureate. He answered his own question even more impudently:

> To *which court*　　The *King's court*
> To *the King's court*　　*Should have the excellence*
> Or *to Hampton Court?*　　*But Hampton Court*
> 　　　　　　　　*Hath the pre-eminence!*

Once again Cavendish, the servant and friend, documents the charges of an enemy. For his enthusiastic description of Wolsey's establishment, of which he had been a leading member, shows not so much a household as a court that was quasi-royal. It numbered 500, which was the same size as the King's household, and it was organized in the same way, from the master cook, resplendent in 'damask, satin or velvet with a chain of gold about his neck', who ran (one supposes at a safe distance) the Cardinal's privy kitchen, to the six gentlemen waiters in his privy chamber who paralleled the same number of gentlemen in the King's.

Similarly with ceremony. The Cardinal's court day, like the King's, centred on his 'coming forth' from his privy chamber to the expectant world without. First, actor to his fingertips, he made sure the audience was ready; then, 'advertised of the furniture of his chambers without with noblemen and gentlemen', the Ipswich boy 'would issue out into them apparelled all in red in the habit of a cardinal'. Before him was borne the Great Seal of England, symbol of the chancellorship, and his cardinal's hat, carried 'by a nobleman or some worthy gentleman right solemnly, bareheaded'. In the presence chamber a regular procession was marshalled, with a sergeant-at-arms carrying a silver-gilt mace, and others bearing two pillars of silver for his cardinalate, and two great crosses of silver, the one for his archbishopric, the other for the legateship that made him the Pope's viceroy in England. The gentlemen ushers cried, 'Oh my lords and masters, make way for my lord's grace!' The throng parted; Wolsey, sniffing his orange pomander, strode through and the attendant dignitaries fell in behind. The procession went through the chambers and into the hall. At the hall door Wolsey mounted his mule; his cross- and pillar-bearers climbed on their horses; four guards with gilt pole-axes formed up round the Cardinal, and he rode out into the street.

A court, of course, needs a king, and Wolsey was no king. But he was a cardinal and a chancellor. He was invested with his cardinal's hat in Westminster Abbey in a ceremony whose solemnity and splendour rivalled 'the coronation of a mighty prince or king'; and he exploited to the full the vice-regal potentialities of the chancellorship. He held the office for life; treated the Great Seal as his personal property and surrounded it with a novel ceremonial. But his pretensions showed most glaringly when he went to the King's court. While he was in the palace his crosses stood in the Presence Chamber, 'on the one side' of the throne and canopy. The latter were the ark of the covenant of monarchy; all doffed their caps before them, and as they did so they paid reverence perforce to the Cardinal's crosses as well.

All said and done, however, Wolsey was only the *alter rex*', the second king. His court, though, in a real sense was the first. When Henry 'came forth', it was only to hear mass in the Chapel Royal; when Wolsey 'issued out', it was to confer with the judges, sit in Chancery, or preside in Star Chamber. Henry's court might be anywhere, and in any case was rarely nearer London than Greenwich. Wolsey's court was usually at York Place, within a few score yards of the Palace of Westminster, the seat of justice, finance and administration. The result was that Henry often had great difficulty in attracting men to his court. He was regularly short of councillors; and sometimes he had 'very few in his Privy Chamber' as Wolsey had taken them too. Even Christmas could be better with the Cardinal. In 1525, for instance, the royal Christmas was so private that it was known as 'the still Christmas'; while Wolsey 'kept open household, to lords, ladies and all other that would come, with plays and disguisings in most royal manner'.

But however much he might eclipse the royal court, Wolsey neglected it at his peril. Henry was still the King, and his affections, though rooted in Wolsey, could still wander. This happened shortly after Wolsey's own rise to supreme power with the emergence of a new group of royal favourites: the minions. Their advent presented the minister with the most serious challenge so far to his power; it also presaged the pattern of politics of the high noon of Henry's reign.

4

THE COURT AND THE CARDINAL

'I CAME TO the court very young', wrote Sir Francis Bryan in his translation of Antonio de Guevara, *A Dispraise of the Life of the Courtier*. As he did so, his mind might well have slipped back nearly twenty-five years to a spring day in 1515. Then the King, 'delighting to set forth young gentlemen', had summoned him and his even younger brother-in-law of four months standing, Nicholas Carew, to be his aids in a 'joust of pleasure'. Henry had picked out other young gentlemen to ride as their opponents, 'and lent to them horses and harness [i.e. armour] to encourage all youth to seek deeds of arms'.

The occasion – a kind of England junior trial – was comparatively modest, without a scrap of cloth of gold. Still, to joust as the King's companions-in-arms was a stunning debut for the two young men whose careers were to be closely intertwined for the next twenty years. Bryan was born into the court: his father was the Queen's Vice-Chamberlain; his mother, the daughter of Lord Berners, the scholarly Governor of Calais, was to be governess to both the Princesses Mary and Elizabeth. Carew, son of the Captain of Calais Castle, had an even better start, and was of Henry's 'own bringing up'. In this exclusive school he had learned three things: good manners, French and jousting. The latter remained an abiding passion: even twenty years later when he was painted by Holbein, it is as a jouster he appears with armour, lance, sword, and a strange, turban-like swathe of cloth on his head. His face is lean, almost ascetic. He stands proud and erect, the hero of innumerable fantastic tournaments.

No portrait survives of Bryan. But we hardly miss it as the man leaps up from the written record. He was a polymath: soldier, sailor, jouster, poet, belletrist, diplomat, intriguer. His character was as various as his career, but tending in everything to extremes. He was charming, lecherous, double-dealing; now crying 'kiss me quick'; now vehemently denouncing sin (but was he serious?). His nickname, half-contemptuous, half-affectionate, was 'the Vicar of Hell'. A restless energy lay at the heart of the man: it made him behave like a twenty-year-old at fifty; consumed him physically until he seemed 'lean and dry without moisture'; and, above all, poured from him in a stream of words. He talked torrentially, brilliantly, scabrously. And he wrote. His poetry, as far as we can reconstruct it, is poor stuff, sententious and didactic. But his prose is wonderful. Antithesis, repetition, climax and the host of other devices that most of his contemporaries learned laboriously and used clumsily came to him as easily as breathing. He did not go to university (that only became fashionable for a gentleman in the next generation); had little Latin and lacked 'knowledge of the [hi]stories, which I do profess is hard for to understand for one of no greater literature than I profess me to be'. Instead he was one of nature's orators.

He was also one of nature's courtiers as, less showily, was his brother-in-law Carew. In the course of the year or two following the debut jousts of 1515 other bright young men began to appear in the royal circle: like Henry Norris, Anthony Knyvet, or William Coffin. In background, tastes and accomplishments they were similar to Carew and

Bryan. But it would be wrong to think of them as mere side-kicks. Most were to forge substantial careers, and some have striking qualities of their own. Norris, for example, always known as 'gentle Mr Norris', had a universal affability, an emollient charm that made him both an effective manager of the Privy Chamber, of which he was head for the decade 1526–36, and probably the best-liked major figure at court. On the other hand, in William Carew we can see, thanks to his recently discovered portrait, the fresh, youthful insouciance that, probably more than anything else, won the King's heart in these years.

For there had been a paradox. Though Henry had come to the throne as a teenage *jeune premier*, his court had remained surprisingly elderly. The 'old' councillors were old indeed at fifty-five or sixty; Wolsey was over forty; and even the noble favourites were in their thirties at least. Now at last, as Cary's elegant French dress, easy pose and flickering half-smile tell us, a new generation had arrived. Their youth seemed to guarantee Henry's own. He was now twenty-five; they were still in their mid-to-late teens – the same age as Henry when he became King. With them time could be held at bay and the long summer afternoon of sport and dalliance could last forever.

Henry's identification with them became complete; they acquired a name, the King's 'minions', that is 'young favourites'; and their position was made public knowledge in the jousts of July 1517. These were no 'junior trial', but a grand tournament, held for the 'solace' of foreign ambassadors at Henry's court. And in pride of place as the King's aides were the young minions; while Carew also had the individual starring role of 'the Blue Knight'. His performance was watched by one of the diplomatic guests, the Venetian envoy Nicolo Sagudino, who described it with an amazement that seems to have been fully justified:

The jousts being ended, a beam was brought, some twenty feet in length, and was placed on the head of one of his Majesty's favourites, by name master Caroll [i.e. Carew], who was one of the jousters, and he ran a long way with the beam on his head to the marvel of everybody.

I suppose the achievements of today's athletes will seem as silly four centuries hence. But Carew was more than a Sebastian Coe. As well as diverting the King's leisure hours, he and the other minions were starting to play an important part in the King's private service. This was in a mess. Henry VII had set up the Privy Chamber to give him solitude to work; Henry VIII, on the other hand, wanted 'pastime with good company'. But instead of reorganizing the private apartments accordingly, he muddled through. The tiny formal establishment of grooms and pages was retained, but many others were welcome in the Privy Chamber: musicians, whose company Henry loved, and, above all, his favourites. In the first years of the reign, Howard, Thomas Knyvet and Brandon must have been with the King till all hours; then it was Carew, Bryan or Norris. For this last group the transition to servant was very easy. The usual finishing school for a young gentleman was a period of service in another household. The minions were young gentlemen in the King's household, what more natural than to make them the King's servants? The road was first taken by Carew. In 1515, when he was just a boy, he was actually made a Groom of the Privy Chamber. But the office was too humble for the appointment to stick. He carried on doing the job all the same: buying goods for the King, and keeping some of the royal plate. Along with Henry Norris he even appeared in lists of the royal establishment.

These 'servants without office' transformed the Privy

Chamber and with it the court. From the beginning a place in the Privy Chamber had conferred the right and duty of perpetual attendance on the King: when he dressed or ate; even when he slept. This had meant little when the Privy Chamber were ciphers. With the minions in position it meant a lot. They had breeding and charm; were brave and athletic, and, above all, had 'the gift of tongues'. In the Privy Chamber they had twenty-four hours a day to direct these qualities on the King. The evidence shows that they took full advantage of the opportunity. Once again, it was Bryan who attracted the attention. Florentius Volusenus, a Scottish humanist who knew him well, remarked casually in retelling a joke that Bryan was 'accustomed to speak familiarly to the King'; while even more strikingly the Abbot of Woburn, under interrogation for treason, stated: 'the said Sir Francis dare boldly speak to the King's Grace the plainness of his mind and that his Grace doth well accept the same'. The words are curiously familiar, for reaching though it does across wide gaps of culture and language, the Abbot's description of Bryan is a faithful paraphrase of Castiglione's own formulation of the purpose and justification of the ideal courtier: 'so to win for himself the mind and favour of the prince he serves that he can and always will tell him the truth about all he needs to know, without fear or risk of displeasing him.'

But of course Bryan and the rest were operating not in Castiglione's idealized Mantua but in Tudor England. And the effect was not to turn Henry's court into a model of virtue but to make it an effective counterweight to Wolsey's. The minions' advantage was proximity to the King; Wolsey's weakness was distance. In the six months following the jousts of 1517, for instance, Wolsey and Henry met once. The 'sweating sickness' had struck in August. Wolsey caught it; suffered repeated bouts, then went off on pilgrimage to Walsingham to recuperate and give thanks for his recovery. Meanwhile Henry, as usual with epidemics, had fled. First he had gone to Windsor. But the sweat followed him, even carrying off 'some of the royal pages who slept in His Majesty's chamber'. Thereafter Henry moved restlessly from house to house, accompanied only by his physician, the Venetian organist Dionysius Memo, and 'three favourite gentlemen'. These were the minions, and for the next few months they and the King formed a second government of England, over and against Wolsey's. The records of the King's government were kept by a clerk of the Chamber and they survive in part. This record, recently rediscovered, is unique. And it is doubly important because it covers the period when the King's government and Wolsey's clashed.

The apple of discord was a woman. Richard Vernon of Haddon Hall in Derbyshire died leaving a widow, Margaret. She was the daughter of Sir Robert Dymoke, the King's hereditary Champion, and was a rich prize. Wolsey wanted her for one of his own servants, Sir William Tyrwhit, and wrote to her accordingly. But one of the minions, William Coffin, had his eye on her too and on 19 November 1517 he trumped Wolsey's letter with one from the King commanding Mrs Vernon to look kindly on *his* suit as one 'whom we singularly favour at this time'. This letter – and a back-up one to Mrs Vernon's neighbour, Geoffrey Foljambe, ordering him to do his bit to help Coffin – had been obtained by Coffin's 'loving fellow', Carew, the favourite of favourites. Characteristically Henry tried to buy Wolsey off with a grant of the wardship of Vernon's heir. But he was not to be appeased: as Sir William Compton, the Groom of the Stool, told Thomas Allen, a London agent of the Earl of Shrewsbury, 'my lord Cardinal is not content withal'. Compton, who disliked Wolsey, evidently enjoyed the story. But for Shrewsbury it was more than idle gossip. He was the local great power in

Derbyshire and Allen's report told him which way to swing. On 19 December Carew wrote to Shrewsbury, gratefully acknowledging his assistance to Coffin, which 'I have shown unto the King's grace to your singular thanks'; whilst Coffin himself assured the Earl that 'whatsoever noise or report is . . . made in those parts to my discomfort . . . the King continueth my good and gracious lord and so will do to the end of the matter'. Coffin's confidence was justified; he got his widow.

'It was', Professor Elton has written, 'the man who could help his servants and friends to advancement under the Crown who mattered in the 350 years between the first Tudor and the last Hanoverian.' In this crucial game the minions had shown that they could beat the minister. But even at the cost of public humiliation Wolsey had learned a crucial lesson. Never would he neglect the royal court again. First, on some pretext or another, he got Carew sent off to the country; then he got his own man in. This was Richard Pace, the royal Secretary.

Pace, a humanist go-getter who rubbed the shine off the glittering prizes in his eagerness to grab them, had just made a leisurely return from a two-year stint as ambassador to the Swiss. Suddenly he catapulted into prominence: in January 1518 the Venetian Ambassador reported that 'the third seat in the secret council has been conferred on him'; in February the scholar was made a gentleman by a grant of arms; and in March he received that inevitable adjunct to greatness in the early sixteenth century: a begging letter from Erasmus. Pace had two jobs at court. One of the things that had opened the way to the Coffin affair was that Wolsey had left Henry with no formal machinery for handling his own letters. Hence the informal correspondence run by the minions. This loop-hole was now blocked by giving Pace the task – which was of course properly the King's Secretary's but rarely in fact discharged by him – of writing the royal letters. His other function was to act as Wolsey's general court agent, processing ministerial papers with the King and reporting on the doings of the court. Ironically one of his first reports informed Wolsey that 'Mr Carew and his wife be returned to the King's grace, too soon after mine opinion'. Once more, Henry had yielded to rival blandishments for, Pace thought, the Carews had come 'by commandment'.

Taming the court was not going to be easy. And the events of 1518 were to make it both harder and more necessary. For the structural reorganization of the court, long overdue, at last took place. This was the result of the first of those bouts of Frenchification that so mark the history of the royal household under Henry VIII. In 1515, François d'Angoulême had succeeded his remote cousin and Mary Tudor's husband, Louis XII, as King Francis I of France. Like Henry he was young and athletic, and like Henry he had built up a circle of royal favourites who were also called the King's minions. Unlike Henry, however, he had created a new post in the royal household specially to accommodate them. Its title – *gentilhomme de la chambre* (i.e. Gentleman of the Chamber) – was obviously chosen to flatter the social pretensions of its intended occupants. At first – despite the appositeness of the precedent – none of this mattered much as relations between England and France, patched up by the marriage of Louis and Mary, had collapsed once more with the accession of the young and warlike Francis. Envious of Francis's first victories in Italy, and worried about their implications, Henry and Wolsey had tried to fight France to the last drop of everybody else's blood – Spanish, German, Swiss, no matter. Their schemes were bungled and by 1518 both sides were ready for a settlement. Francis wanted peace in the north to free his hands for war in Italy, while mounting financial problems made England accommodating about the terms.

A grand French embassy arrived in September to fix the final details. Prominent in its train were Francis I's leading *gentilshommes de la chambre*. Their arrival presented the English government with a dilemma. Obviously they should be paired off in processions and the like with Henry's own minions. The latter, on the other hand, held no formal office and so could not claim equality of status with their French counterparts. The dilemma was solved by borrowing the French post of *gentilhomme de la chambre* for the English royal household and appointing the minions to it *en masse*. The only difficulty was the name. The continued existence of the English Chamber as a separate household department made an exact translation of the French impossible, but after a few false starts the definitive form of Gentleman of the Privy Chamber appeared by 1520.

1517 had shown what the minions could do without the status of formal office. Now they had it, anything could happen. The actual issue seems to have been the minions' pro-French inclination in foreign policy. This was a clear result of circumstance. Their office, whose very title was French, had been established in response to the arrival of the French embassy of September 1518. And immediately afterwards the leading minions had paid a return visit to the French court. There Francis I had lavished charm and favour on them. They were adopted into the circle of French minions and joined in their boisterous pastimes: for example, the minions of both nations 'with the French King rode . . . disguised through Paris, throwing eggs, stones and other foolish trifles at the people'. All of which went to their heads. When the minions returned to England,

they were all French, in eating, drinking and apparell;
yea and in French vices and brags. So that all the

*estates of England were by them laughed at; the ladies
and gentlewomen were dispraised, so that nothing by
them was praised but if it were after the French turn.*

And what began as youthful infatuation in most cases
turned into a deep Francophilia that was as important cul-
turally as it was politically. For Wolsey this was irritating
at least as he wished to be able to manoeuvre Henry freely
between Francis I and the latter's archrival, Charles V.
Charles, the youngest member of the 'triumvirate of kings'
who dominated Europe in the first half of the sixteenth
century, was just completing his succession to the most
stunning of family inheritances. He had become, while still
a boy, Duke of Burgundy on the premature death of his
father, the Archduke Philip, in 1506; ten years later he had
made good his claims to succeed his maternal grandfather,
Ferdinand of Aragon, in the twin Spanish kingdoms of
Aragon and Castile; and finally, in June 1519, he was to be
elected Emperor after the death the previous January of his
other grandfather, Maximilian. The odds against assem-
bling and holding such far-flung dominions were
considerable, but once they were overcome, the gawky,
lantern-jawed Charles was manifestly the heavy-weight of
Europe.

In one sense, therefore, the manoeuvres of the German
princes in the much fought-over Imperial election, in which
Francis I tried to buy votes for himself like an Irish-
American mayor, stacked the cards against Francophile
minions. But in another perspective, foreign policy, as
patronage had been before, was only a symptom of a larger
problem. This was shrewdly observed by the Venetian
agent Giustiniani. Wolsey, he suggested, perceived the
minions 'to be so intimate with the King that in the course
of time they might have ousted him from the government'.
Faced by so direct a threat to his influence over the King's

mind – the foundation of his power – the minister struck first.

In May 1519 most of the minions, with a few lesser favourites, were expelled from court. No formal criminal charges were preferred against them. Instead they were simply denounced before the Council for unbecoming conduct: for encouraging the King to gamble; for treating him with undue familiarity; in short, for being 'youths of evil counsel, and intent on their own benefit to the detriment, hurt and discredit' of the King. Three of those expelled were appointed to leading posts at Calais (the early-Tudor India); to the remainder Henry gave 'employment *extra curiam* (i.e. outside the court) in other parts of the kingdom'.

Probably the accusations against the minions were true or partly true, though the King himself was at least as guilty as his supposed corrupters. But the truth or false-hood of the charges is really beside the point. What matters is to know how in this first catastrophe to befall his favourites, as in all the succeeding ones, Henry was brought to accept or even to further the removal of those closest and dearest to him. And the answer in 1519, as it usually was later, was manipulation – in this case by Wolsey. Hitherto, as we have seen, the Cardinal had ruled by encouraging Henry to indulge in pastimes and pleasures. With the rise of the minions, however, this technique became double-edged: the more Wolsey left Henry free to enjoy himself, the more time he spent with the minions and the greater their influence grew. Clearly, a new tactic was needed.

It was introduced at the beginning of 1519. Suddenly the air was thick with proposals for reform of everything from the Privy Purse to the state of the economy, the administration of justice, the Exchequer, Ireland and vagrancy. The schemes ranged as widely in approach as in content, but all had one feature in common: they were designed to absorb as much of the King's time and attention as possible. In other words Wolsey, who was certainly the author of the schemes, had changed front completely. If the companions of Henry's pleasures were now his principal rivals, then the King must be plunged into affairs of state. There was, however, no point in trying to interest him in routine. Instead things had to be dressed up with the tinsel of exciting proposals for reform. Once these caught the King's attention, however fleetingly, the minions could be painted as worthless and dangerous wastrels, good for nothing but to divert Henry, the father of his people, from his self-imposed labours for the commonwealth. And so it happened. But as soon as the minions were gone Wolsey's interest in reform dropped sharply. The Privy Purse (which was run – it should be remembered – by Sir William Compton, whom the minister hated) was put on a more regular and much more limited footing, and the administration of the King's Wards (where Wolsey had suffered some sharp patronage defeats at the hands of the minions) was tidied up. For the rest, though, Palsgrave's damning verdict is just: 'Every one of these enterprises was great, and the least of them to our commonwealth much expedient . . . but they have been begun, and brought to no good end.'

So in the first struggle between the minister and the Privy Chamber the former emerged triumphant. But the triumph – in its absolute form at least – was short-lived. Nor is it hard to see why. The expulsion of the minions had left four empty places in the Privy Chamber. In the first flush of his victory Wolsey was able to fill these at his pleasure. Naturally the men he chose – Sir Richard Wingfield, Sir Richard Weston, Sir Richard Jerningham and Sir William Kingston – were his loyal adherents. But they were also chosen because they would fit the new, hard-working persona that Wolsey was imposing on the King: all four were serious, successful careerists in middle age at least. So long as Wolsey persisted in his schemes for reform, this suited well enough. But when the minister's pressure slackened, Henry reverted quickly to his old habits. And for these the four distinguished but dull 'Knights of the Body in the Privy Chamber', as they were christened, were sorely inadequate. Accordingly, the minions – so temptingly near in honourable exile – were recalled, and by the autumn of 1519 they had regained both their places in the Privy Chamber and all their old ascendancy at court.

They celebrated this recovery of the royal favour in the masque of 3 September 1519 at the palace of New Hall, near Chelmsford in Essex. The four Knights of the Body appeared as ridiculous old buffers in the humorous farce or 'antimasque' with which the entertainment began; while the King and the minions inhabited the gracious world of eternal youth that formed the masque proper. So just as the disposition of the forces in the joust of July 1517 had set the seal on the minions' domination of the court, the distinction between masque and antimasque in September 1519 symbolized the new party structure of the court. Wolsey's appointees remained in the Privy Chamber, but only on the penumbra of royal favour, while the minions enjoyed, as before, a flamboyant intimacy with the King. The future pattern of factional division in the Privy Chamber between a ministerial party and its court opponents was clearly foreshadowed.

While this struggle with the court was going on, Wolsey was also engaged in another, parallel battle. One of the reform memoranda of c.1519 is headed 'Privy Remembrance', and begins with a proposal for the King 'to put himself in strength with his most trusty servants in every shire for the surety of his royal person and succession and resisting of all manner bandings'. The other reform schemes suggest business; this one breathes fear, with mysterious precautions against obscure dangers. Business was Wolsey's weapon against the minions; fear was his instrument against his other enemies, the nobility.

Henry, of course, had begun his reign as patron of a noble reaction: together King and nobles had turned against the legacy of Henry VII, and together they had ridden against the French. Inevitably the rise of Wolsey soured all that, and by 1516 charges of illegal retaining reminiscent of those of Henry VII were being pressed against a large group of nobles. But the atmosphere of universal suspicion came only later. The seeds were planted by Wolsey, and in April 1519 Pace conveyed Henry's thanks to the Cardinal for remarks in his last letter 'touching great personages'. But Henry proved an apt pupil. Soon he was tricking nobles into coming to court with small retinues, and within a few months his anxieties were so acute that he wrote Wolsey a secret note in his own hand, ordering him to 'make good watch on the Duke of Suffolk, on the Duke of Buckingham, on my Lord of Northumberland, on my Lord of Derby, on my Lord of Wiltshire, and on other which you think suspect'.

Particularly striking is the inclusion of the Duke of Suffolk, Charles Brandon. Brandon, the intimate friend of Knyvet and Howard, had been the residuary legatee of Henry's first group of favourites, and it was this which carried him to his dukedom in 1514. His dukedom, and still more his half-welcome marriage to the King's sister, inevitably changed his position. But his evolution from favourite to magnate was completed by the rise of the minions. They now took over Suffolk's old place as the King's squires and companions, while Suffolk graduated to the captaincy of the opposing band of knights in the jousts of July 1517. The position was honourable but dangerous, as the Duke of Buckingham well knew when he wrote to

Wolsey that 'he would rather go to Rome' than joust against Henry. The suspicions round Suffolk intensified in the next few months. But, knowing both Henry and Wolsey as he did, he cleared himself by prostrate submission.

Buckingham was neither so sensible nor so flexible. He had hoped for much from Henry's succession; was correspondingly embittered when his hopes were disappointed, and, worst of all, gave free vent to his disappointment. What he did not do, however, was to build up his own court faction. Some of the later articles drawn up against him could be read in this light – like the charge that he 'hath always done as much as he could to have favour of the King's guard'; or that he had bought the 'good will' of the King's favourite, Sir Edward Neville, with 'a doublet of cloth of silver'. But weightier matters tell against. Buckingham had a running quarrel with Compton, the Groom of the Stool, and bore a special grudge against the minions, grumbling because the King 'would give his fees, offices and rewards rather to boys than to noblemen'. Compton and the minions, of course, had their own bones to pick with Wolsey, and a better politician than Buckingham would have done everything to make common cause with them. But Buckingham disdained such allies. Instead, in his foolish pride, he consigned King, Cardinal and court to a common perdition and turned, as he had done at the beginning of the reign, to the collective power of his order. 'It would do well enough', he said, 'if noblemen durst break their minds together.'

So politically, as in every other way, Buckingham was reactionary not innovative. Rather than making a faction within the court he was trying, like a fifteenth-century king-maker, to raise a noble party against the court: then, if he 'might have had a convenient time, and have been strong enough to have made his party good, he would have done as much against the King's grace as he could have done'. But whatever form of politicking the Duke resorted to, he was bad at it. He talked too much and did too little and words and actions alike served only to provide Henry and Wolsey with plausible charges to undo him. He was summoned to court early in April 1521 and shadowed on his way thither by Compton and other courtiers with detachments of the Guard. Finally, once the trap had safely snapped shut, he was arrested in his barge on the Thames on the 16th. Trial followed swiftly, and he was arraigned for high treason in Westminster Hall on 13 May. His own servants testified against him; the Duke of Norfolk, presiding as Lord High Steward for the day, asked his peers whether he were guilty and wrote the answers down. In each case it was the same, 'he says that he is guilty'. Four days later he was beheaded.

Buckingham's fall reverberated throughout the courts of Europe. But on the English court it had little effect. Here instead it was business as usual between Wolsey and the minions. Their return in 1519 had proved more digestible than might have been expected. This was because England's foreign relations, which had triggered the establishment of the office of Gentleman of the Privy Chamber, now intervened again. But this time their effect was to offer the minister a subtler way of controlling his opponents in the Privy Chamber than expulsion.

The years after the Treaty of Universal Peace of 1518 witnessed an elaborate diplomatic minuet as England leaned this way and that between the rival great powers of Francis I of France and Charles V of the Empire, Spain and the Netherlands. More and more openly, however, Henry inclined to the Empire, finally declaring war on France in 1522.

The war and the antecedent diplomacy had a major impact on the court, and hence on politics. War needs commanders; diplomacy, ambassadors. And from 1520 to 1525 both were supplied, very largely, from the Gentlemen of the Privy Chamber: they dominated the crucial French embassy, the Channel fleets, and the major expedition of 1523 against the Scots (who, as usual, the French egged on as a diversionary tactic).

There were, of course, good reasons for the extracurial employment of the Gentlemen. Partly, it was that the King could trust them completely; at least as important, however, was their ability to represent him with special vigour and force. Because of their extraordinarily intimate contact with the King's physical body, something of the royal unction rubbed off onto them, so that their persons stood in a sense for the King's own. This meant that their presence in the army had something of the morale-raising effect of the King's acting directly as commander-in-chief of his troops; while their employment as ambassadors was an effective substitute for the summit conferences which were the age's preferred form of diplomacy.

But though there could be no dispute about the importance of employing the Gentlemen away from court, contemporaries accused Wolsey of perverting evident necessity into a mere excuse to remove his enemies – actual or potential – from about the King. Palsgrave levelled the charge in its most extreme form, alleging that the Cardinal had 'undone all the young gentlemen of England that served us and sent some beyond the sea on embassies and devised means to linger them there still . . . because we would have them out of the way.' Polydore Vergil is more specific. He claims that the despatch of Sir William Compton, the Groom of the Stool, on the Scottish expedition of 1523 was arranged 'at Wolsey's instigation, so that the latter might gradually cause him to be hateful to Henry' during his absence.

The charges – though unprovable – are probably true.

But why the Gentlemen were employed as they were is relatively unimportant; what really matters are the manifest consequences of that employment in dispeopling the court. In fact, in the early 1520s so many of the Privy Chamber were absent from court for so long that at times the King, as he vigorously complained, was almost destitute of body servants. One such occasion came in September 1521, when Henry informed Wolsey by Richard Pace that 'he hath now very few to give attendance upon his person in his Privy Chamber'; accordingly, he requested that the two Gentlemen whom the Cardinal had taken with him to the conference at Calais might be sent back to court. Whether Wolsey had deliberately engineered this situation or not, he cannot have regretted it: an empty Privy Chamber meant that the minister's monopoly of patronage and counsel went unchallenged.

But this fortunate state of affairs could not last forever. England's performance in the war was not distinguished and Charles V's overwhelming victory at Pavia enabled him to dispense with his exhausted ally altogether. Wolsey and Henry did their best to pick up the pieces by a complete change of front. By the Treaty of The More, signed in August 1525, France, England's ancient enemy, became her chosen ally. And with the Treaty, the second great era of war of Henry's reign was ended.

Peace forced Wolsey to return to the methods of 1519 to keep the Privy Chamber under control. But it was a return with a difference. Once again the rhetoric of reform was used to bend Henry to Wolsey's purposes; this time, however, the rhetoric actually led to action, at least as far as the household was concerned.

In January 1526 – a mere five months after the signing of the peace treaty – the great reforming household Ordinances of Eltham were published. But if the timing of the reforms was determined by the advent of peace, their purpose (at least their ostensible purpose) was to cope with the impact of the late war. This had affected the household in two main ways. First, by demanding the service of so many of the household away from the court, it had gravely dislocated the organization of the household itself. And second, by breaking the royal finances, it had made a reduction in the cost, and hence the size, of the household imperative. The two problems differed greatly in difficulty.

The administrative reform of the household proceeded swiftly, on paper at least: by late 1525 separate orders had been published for the Household proper and the Chamber, and possibly for the Privy Chamber as well. Here the only real novelty was the recognition that, since the last major household ordinance of about 1495, the Privy Chamber had become a fully-fledged department of the household, co-equal and perhaps more with the other two. The second goal of the reforms – the reduction in the household's establishment – was also relatively unproblematical for the Household and Chamber: few of their personnel, and none who were to be cut, were politically significant, so the provision of pensions was enough to secure their removal. For the Privy Chamber, however, the story is very different. They were too important to be pensioned off summarily; nor did their conduct offer Wolsey the same grounds for procuring their ignominious dismissal as in 1519. Instead, they had to be bought out at a price commensurate with their massive political leverage.

Here Wolsey was in luck. The promotion of Sir Thomas Boleyn to the peerage in June 1525 freed one major office, and the death of Sir Richard Wingfield in July another, as well as a host of minor posts. The problem was to stop Henry doling them out piecemeal as usual. This Wolsey managed by a sharp reminder in September of Henry's 'intended purpose' (that is, household reform). Then followed several weeks of hard bargaining, in which other distinguished royal servants were caught up willy-nilly. Sir Thomas More, for example, was required to exchange the Undertreasurership of England for Wingfield's old office of Chancellor of the Duchy of Lancaster. This resulted in his heavy financial loss, but Wolsey was determined to block Compton's hopes of the Chancellorship and a seat on the Council. By Christmas the negotiations were complete and the minister drew up in his own hand – such was the importance and secrecy of the task – the list of *quid pro quos* that were to be offered to those members of the Privy Chamber who were marked down for dismissal. Probably under some duress the victims accepted, and the way was open for the triumphant proclamation of the reforms.

The King had kept Christmas with a much reduced household in the comparatively small palace of Eltham. There he was joined by Wolsey, and in the first three weeks of January the Eltham Ordinances were promulgated. Essentially they were a fusion: they brought together the separate departmental reforming orders of the previous autumn and the reduced list of the Privy Chamber's establishment that Wolsey had forced through over Christmas. And a glance at this list (which appears in Chapter 55 of the Ordinances) shows the extent of Wolsey's victory. The number of Gentlemen had been reduced from about twelve to six, and in the process both Wolsey's rather ineffective supporters and his leading enemies (Compton, the Groom of the Stool, Carew and Bryan, the two most important sometime minions, and George Boleyn, Anne's brother and the King's personal page) had been removed. The survivors were cautious neutrals, like Henry Norris, the new Groom of the Stool, who had picked their way through the minefield of competing interests that was the court with a universal smile. But of course a Privy Chamber staffed by neutrals was a Privy Chamber depoliticized: in other words, by a highly selective response to a genuine need for economy Wolsey had managed to shift the department that had been his greatest rival for political power from the political arena altogether.

But Wolsey's victory had only been won at a price. Almost certainly, the apparently anomalous Chapter 74 of the Ordinances, which set up a Council attendant on the King that looks remarkably like the fully-fledged Privy Council instituted in 1540, was the other side of the bargain. If the minister were to be given a free hand with the Privy Chamber, then his fellow politicians were determined that a more formalized Council should put some sort of limit on his otherwise untrammelled power. In the event, however, pressure of circumstances combined with the Cardinal's cunning to bring the scheme to nothing. Instead, the brake on Wolsey's power (and eventually the breaking of it) came, as it always had done, not from the administrative machinery of government but from the court.

5

ANNE BOLEYN

The Beginnings of Faction

SHE 'KEPT HER MAIDS . . . so occupied in sewing and working of shirts and smocks for the poor, that [never] was there any leisure to follow such pastimes as daily are seen now-a-days to reign in princes' courts'. That was how her silk woman remembered the court of Anne Boleyn. The picture hardly fits with A. F. Pollard's view that Anne appealed only 'to the less refined part of Henry's nature'. But then everything about her challenges stereotypes.

Sixteenth-century women were supposed to be silent and demure: like Cordelia, whose voice 'was ever soft, gentle and low – an excellent thing in woman'. Anne, on the other hand, was brilliant, talkative and assertive. Her unconventionality swept Henry off his feet. Always he had been surrounded by people saying 'yes'; now at last someone dared to say 'no'. The trouble was that she continued to say 'no' after they were married and the novelty of that wore off quickly. Others got still rougher treatment. She drove the Duke of Norfolk from the room with 'words that you wouldn't use to a dog'. And, like whipped curs, the nobles of England slunk off to Eustache Chapuys, the Imperial Ambassador and Anne's inveterate enemy, to grouse at 'her arrogance and spite'. Her fall was greeted with delight, but even her worst enemy had to pay tribute to her 'sense, wit and courage'.

Strength of mind is not too surprising in a royal mistress; her other principal characteristic is, however. Anne was not the unthinking vehicle of the Reformation – the pretty face that dissolved a thousand monasteries. Instead she had strong religious opinions of her own. To call her 'Lutheran', as did Chapuys, perhaps goes too far. On the other hand she was certainly a convinced 'evangelical', with a passionate commitment to the scriptures as the very 'word of God'. She distributed improving books; read them ostentatiously herself, and, since translations of the scriptures were still banned in England, arranged for their importation from France. Preachers of the 'word' benefited too, and Anne 'was a special comforter and aider of the professors of Christ's gospel'. She helped promote two of the great names of the Reformation, Thomas Cranmer and Hugh Latimer, to the bench of bishops, and gave much-needed assistance to a host of lesser scholars.

Catherine of Aragon, Henry's first Queen, was a woman of distinction too. She was more deeply learned than Anne; just as religious, and infinitely more regal. But it was Anne's very unwomanishness that made her so effective. She functioned, like her daughter Elizabeth, as an honorary man. She was one politician among others, and was judged as such without any sense of incongruity by her panegyrist John Foxe, author of the *Book of Martyrs*. All went well for the gospel, he wrote, while Henry VIII had 'council about him' like Anne, or Cromwell, or Cranmer. On the other hand, of course, though Anne handled power like a man, she had got it – if not through witchcraft as Henry later professed to believe – then certainly through female wiles.

How she perfected them, like other things about her early career, is at last becoming clearer. She was born in about 1501, the daughter of Sir Thomas Boleyn and his first wife Elizabeth, daughter of the Duke of Norfolk. In

1513 she was sent off to the Archduchess Margaret, Regent of the Netherlands, to learn French and get the polish of one of the most sophisticated courts in northern Europe. She made an excellent impression and Margaret wrote to her father that she found her 'so poised and pleasant' that all the thanks were on her side. Anne was summoned back in 1514 to accompany Henry's sister Mary on her journey to become Queen of France. And, no doubt because of her proficiency in the language, she was one of a handful of English servants that Louis XII allowed his tearful wife to keep. She would come back to England with the widowed and remarried Mary in 1515, but probably travelled with her father to the French court when he went there as ambassador in 1519. His stint lasted only twelve months, but she stayed on until early 1522. Then, as war once more came near, she returned home along with the English students at the Sorbonne.

By education, then, Anne was wholly French. Three lengthy visits had given her a 'great affection and perfect love . . . for the French tongue', and so refined her behaviour that even a Frenchman thought that no one would take her for 'English by her manners, but a fine French woman born'. This may seem a strange upbringing for the mother of Queen Elizabeth I, who was to boast she was 'mere English'. But Boleyn was a shrewd careerist and knew what he was doing. By the second decade of Henry's reign, to be fashionable meant to be French. The treaty of September 1518 was the turning point. That month Henry Frenchified his private service and made the French minions who were hostages for the performance of the treaty honoured guests at his court. They taught their hosts how things were done in Paris, while Henry's minions were learning the same lesson at first hand on their visit to Francis I. The expulsion of the minions was a setback for these developments, but a very temporary one. The result was that Anne came back to a court that might have been designed as the perfect stage for her talents. Everybody was trying to be French; she was French.

All that was needed was the entrée to these circles of high fashion. Her father, now Treasurer of the Household, could do much; her sister Mary could do more. For on 4 February 1520 she had married the handsome young William Cary, Gentleman of the Privy Chamber, in the presence of the King himself. The marriage took her into the inner court: she was lodged with her husband in a chamber near the King; received royal New Year's gifts and took part in masques. And it was in one of these, in March 1522, that Anne made her debut in company with her sister.

That unfortunately is the last hard piece of information about her for five crucial years. But sometime, and probably sooner rather than later, she came to general notice. Sir Thomas Wyatt writes as though all the young puppy dogs of the court were baying at her heels, with himself as the one 'that furthest cometh behind'. Also in hot pursuit was Lord Henry Percy, heir of the Earl of Northumberland, who was warned off by Wolsey for his pains. But when Henry himself caught the scent it is impossible to be sure. It is unclear too how she reacted. But his early letters to her suggest that he was made to work hard. (These letters, by the way, are in French, and for some inscrutable reason have finished up in the Vatican Library.) Finally, 'having been more than a year wounded by the dart of love, and not yet sure whether I shall fail, or find a place in your affection', Henry put the question to her directly. Was she prepared 'to do the office of a true, loyal mistress, and give yourself, body and heart, to me'? If she were, he promised faithfully to 'make you my sole mistress, remove all others from my affection, and serve you only'. She accepted. But in return she offered only her heart. Her body would not come until the King had married her, or was irretrievably committed to doing so.

Anne was not, of course, Henry's first mistress. Her sister Mary had been one (her son Henry, born in 1525, was commonly supposed the King's); and Elizabeth Blount, mother of the King's acknowledged bastard, the Duke of Richmond, had been another. But two things were different this time. The first was Anne herself. She was not a nice girl, like Elizabeth Blount; nor a silly slut like her sister. Instead she was experienced enough to play the sexual game as Henry's equal. But she would not have dared to set the stakes so high if circumstances had not been different too. It was now clear that Catherine of Aragon would never give Henry a son and he wanted – needed – one desperately.

Thus the bombshell of the divorce that broke in 1527. Its immediate effect on the court was to undo Wolsey's elaborate scheme of reform of 1526. This in any case, like many other aspects of his policy, had been both over-ambitious and incomplete. Its neutralization of the Privy Chamber was incomplete because at the last minute the King had insisted on retaining his cousin, the Marquess of Exeter, whom Wolsey regarded as an enemy, in the department. So as a counterpoise the Cardinal put in one of the most courtly and distinguished of his own adherents, Sir John Russell, later Earl of Bedford. And the scheme was over-ambitious, or at least impracticable, because it rested on the unlikely assumption that the remaining Gentlemen would be prepared to abide by the stringent limitations on their political activities that were set out in the Eltham Ordinances. These, in a section added at the last minute by Wolsey, commanded that the servants of the Privy Chamber should bear:

humble, reverent, secret and lowly service about all

*such things as [the King's] pleasure shall be to depute
and put them to do; not pressing his Grace, nor
advancing themselves, either in further service than his
Grace will or shall assign them unto; or also in suits,
or intermeddle of any causes or matters whatsoever
they be.*

Some of the Privy Chamber, and perhaps they were the
wiser, were content to operate within these rules, but most
were not. The result was that within the Privy Chamber the
political temperature rose as latent ambition combined
with the incipient party division represented by the dis-
ruptive presence of Exeter and Russell. Outside the department feelings ran even higher, thanks to the determination
of most of the expelled Gentlemen to recover their coveted
places about the King.

To these varieties of ambition the rise of Anne Boleyn
was a godsend. Hitherto Wolsey had always been able,
when it came to the crunch, to win Henry round to his way
of thinking. Now, though, there was a mistress to whom
Henry had vowed the sole place in his heart, 'removing all
other from his affection'. That certainly meant Catherine
of Aragon; it might also mean Wolsey. The Cardinal
understood the implications immediately and started to
pack the Privy Chamber with clients like Sir Richard Page,
his former chamberlain, and Thomas Heneage, lately the
head of Wolsey's own privy chamber. Anne replied by
restoring supporters of her own, like her cousin Sir Francis
Bryan and her brother George Boleyn, to their former
offices in the department. While even adherents of
Catherine of Aragon, like Sir Nicholas Carew, managed,
with the sudden weakening of the Cardinal's control, to get
their jobs back too. In the course of a few months in
1527–8 the Privy Chamber had repoliticized.

It was like going back eleven years to the summer of

1517. In 1528, too, the 'sweat' kept King and minister apart for long periods, and an issue of patronage became a bone of contention. The Abbess of Wilton, a fashionable and aristocratic nunnery, had died. Anne Boleyn put in a bid for her sister-in-law, Eleanor Cary (whose brother William had been one of the most prominent victims of the sweat); on the other hand, Wolsey, after a feint of supporting Dame Eleanor, backed Dame Isabella Jordan, Prioress of Sion. He successfully black-balled Eleanor on grounds of her 'dissolute living'; but Henry, to pacify Anne and her friends in the Privy Chamber, said that Dame Isabella should not be appointed either. Nevertheless Wolsey did so. Perhaps he had decided to make a test case for his power; perhaps he thought Henry would forgive and forget. In any case he made a terrible miscalculation. Wolsey's enemies in the Privy Chamber had a field day, and all his supporters, like Heneage and Russell, could do was warn him of what was coming and try to soften the blow. That was not easy, since Henry sent a letter that seared the paper. It was not, the King wrote, 'the right train of a trusty, loving friend and servant' to his master to appoint 'a person which was by him defended [i.e. forbidden]'. But worse, Henry continued, had been Wolsey's attempts to excuse his offence by pleas of ignorance. He exploded the plea by verbatim quotation of his Secretary's letters; then delivered the *coup de grâce*:

> *Ah! my lord, it is a double offence, both to do ill and to colour it too; but with men that hath wit it cannot be accepted so. Wherefore, good my lord, use no more that way with me, for there is no man living that more hateth it.*

With much grovelling on Wolsey's side things were smoothed over. But the seeds of doubt had been sown.

So it was a return with a difference. A decade earlier an affronted Wolsey had been able to expel the minions from court; and only two years before, in 1526, he had been able to buy them out. He even tried similar ploys now, and when a Gentleman of the Privy Chamber, Sir Thomas Cheyney, 'had offended the legate some days past, . . . [he] was for that reason put out of court'. But all Cheyney needed to do was to run to Anne, who 'put him in again, in spite of the Cardinal, not without using rude words to Wolsey'. The rules of the game had changed. Wolsey, unable to purge the court, could no longer rule in solitary state over and against the court; instead he had to come off his pedestal and become one court-faction leader among others.

In the Privy Chamber the pattern of faction followed naturally from the highly political appointments and reappointments of 1527–8. First there were the minister's supporters, Russell, Heneage and Page. Second were his old court opponents, led by Carew and his close associate the Marquess of Exeter. These – the former minions – had matured into convinced conservatives, whose youthful contempt for Wolsey had been given a new edge of passion by their intense personal devotion to Catherine of Aragon and her daughter, the Princess Mary. And third were the adherents of the rising star of Anne Boleyn, who made up perhaps the strongest of the factions. They were led by Anne's brother George, who was created Viscount Rochford in 1529, and Sir Francis Bryan, the ex-minion, who had broken with his fellows on the issue of the divorce. George, who was very close to his sister, had many of Anne's talents and all of her pride; while Bryan used his privilege 'boldly [to] speak to the King's grace the plainness of his mind' to devastating effect. Writing to Henry from Rome, where he had been sent to hold a watching brief on the negotiations for the divorce, he dropped deadly hints

79

about Wolsey's loyalty: 'Whosoever hath made your grace believe that [the Pope] would do for you in this cause, hath not, as I think, done your grace the best service'. While on his way through France he had picked up leads from Francis I that were later to turn into full-blown charges of treason against the Cardinal. The other members of the Boleyn faction were hardly of the same weight, and one, Sir Francis Weston, the King's favourite page, was frankly a butterfly. But Cheyney and William Brereton were major figures in the local politics of Kent and Cheshire respectively; and still more importantly Henry Norris, the Groom of the Stool and the man closest to Henry's heart in these years, while not exactly a partisan, leant as far in Anne's direction as his good sense and innate balance allowed.

The Council, now meeting more-and-more at court, split similarly. Wolsey, when he was present, fought his own corner; her brother George and her father, now Earl of Wiltshire, were Anne's partisans; whilst Exeter and More did what they could for Catherine. But there was a further element here. As Wolsey's star waned, the nobility, personified in the two leaders of the order, the Dukes of Norfolk and Suffolk, went into the ascent. Broadly the two dukes allied themselves with Anne, but they always had their own fish to fry. These groupings in court and Council were divided, of course, not only over personalities, but also over policies. The two great issues of the day were the divorce and the continuation of Wolsey's ministry. The Wolseians supported both; the Aragonese opposed both; while the Boleyns and their noble allies supported the former and opposed the latter. And in the centre, at the focus of these diverse pressures, stood the King himself: deeply and personally interested in the outcome of policy, yet apparently incapable of determining its direction himself. For the moment it was stalemate.

Stalemate was one of the faces of faction politics; the other was sudden crisis. Faction politics had appeared, much against Wolsey's will, in 1527–8. The first crisis of faction followed swiftly in 1529 with himself as its victim.

The crisis was provoked by events outside the control of anybody in England. On 21 June 1529 the Imperialists routed the French at the battle of Landriano and the two sides made ready to come to terms at the Peace of Cambrai. That ended the last faint chance that the Pope could be got to agree to the divorce between Henry and the Emperor's aunt Catherine. And that in turn destroyed Wolsey, who had staked everything on a papal dissolution of Henry's marriage. He now stood 'naked to my enemies'. And all of these – Boleyns, Aragonese, nobles – sank their own fundamental differences and went into alliance against him. Together they worked on Henry's temporary dis-illusionment with his minister, and the pressure, coupled with Anne's skilful management of her lover, was enough to break the trust of almost twenty years and destroy Wolsey. But once Wolsey's fall was accomplished (and once, above all, he was safely hounded to the natural death that cheated his enemies of the opportunity to execute him), the triumphant coalition had no further grounds for unity. The time, in other words, was ripe for a further realignment. And this was possible thanks to the survival of the Wolsey group at court. Despite their master's fall and their own varying reactions to it, the worst they had suffered was a few unsubstantiated threats from Anne. Their own unity remained; moreover they had found a new leader in Thomas Cromwell, Wolsey's former legal factotum.

6

THOMAS CROMWELL

Rule by Faction

IT WOULD BE HARD to think of two more strongly
contrasted portraits than Wolsey's and Cromwell's.
Wolsey appears all in scarlet; Cromwell, all in black. And
the temptation is to paint the contrast between their
ministries equally strongly. In such a scenario Wolsey was
the last medieval churchman to rule England; Cromwell
the first modern bureaucrat-minister (after all, does not
Holbein even paint him with books and papers before him
and a letter in his hand?). Neither pole of the antithesis
stands up to scrutiny. Wolsey, far from being a typical
ecclesiastical minister, was an *alter rex* and as such quite
individual; and his style, far from being 'medieval', was
the arch-embodiment of Renaissance rhetoric. While
Cromwell, far from repudiating Wolsey, went out of his
way to express both continuity and gratitude by taking the
chief of Wolsey's coat-of-arms – or a rose gules between
two Cornish choughs sable – and making it the fesse of his
own.

And the similarities were more than heraldic.
Cromwell's origins, like Wolsey's, were humble and his
earlier career unsettled and untypical. Both men, also, had
an insatiable appetite for hard work, and both were overwhelming and charming in equal measure. Finally,
Cromwell was at least as much a master of rhetoric as

Wolsey: later scholarship has analysed his unusually latinate and innovative vocabulary; while even the Register of the Garter broke its official tone to note that when Cromwell received the Order in 1540 he gave thanks 'with all the eloquence he was master of (and certainly he was master of the justest)'. And this rhetorical awareness meant that – in the fullness of time – he tended to handle the King in much the same way as his predecessor. Wolsey, it may be remembered, had lubricated the King with curios and objects of virtu; Cromwell, on the other hand, seems to have tapped the King's love of mechanical devices by the gift of the sixteenth-century equivalent of executive toys. In January 1536, for example, Ralph Sadler, Cromwell's trusty servant, reported that during an audience with Henry which was largely devoted to the arrangements following Catherine of Aragon's welcome death he had 'delivered unto his Grace your lock and opened unto him all the gins of the same, which his Grace liketh marvellously well and heartily thanked you for the same'.

But the differences, if not of the type conventionally assumed, were no less striking. In part this was a result of contrasts in character: Wolsey loved pomp and circumstance; Cromwell was unusually indifferent to the outward show of power. At the same time, however, he was much more aware of its realities: while his claims as a religious or social reformer are still debatable, about his success in increasing the royal power and revenues there can be no doubt whatever. And, above all, Cromwell was both a more ruthless politician and probably a more subtle one as well.

All this matters; but the key distinctions were not personal but structural. Wolsey ruled in solitary eminence as 'the King's friend'. Everything else flowed from this: his personal pomp and his attitude to the court, to his own servants and above all to faction. Faction, as we have seen repeatedly, had no place in his scheme of things; it was thrust upon him only by the rise of Anne Boleyn. For Cromwell the opposite is the case.

He started his ministry where Wolsey had finished his. The foundations of his second career in the royal service lay in the discretion with which he had tidied up the wreck of his old master's fortunes. In that operation Russell, Heneage and Page, his former colleagues in Wolsey's service, had been useful allies; once Cromwell emerged as Wolsey's probable successor they became his loyal dependants. From the very beginning, therefore, Cromwell was the leader (admittedly from outside) of a Privy Chamber faction in a fully factionalized court. And, again unlike Wolsey, he showed himself a supreme master of the bloody game of faction politics.

All this meant that Cromwell's power was more institutionalized, less personal than the Cardinal's. But the institution it depended on was not the bureaucracy or Council but the court. This fact, like its contrary under his predecessor, governed his attitude to his servants: he regarded them as the necessary instruments of his rule and consequently trusted them more and rewarded them more than Wolsey had ever done his. It also conditioned his relatively modest way of life: in part this was the result of a certain natural austerity, but it was also a recognition that his source of power lay not in his own household so much as in his control of the personnel of the inner apartments of the court, and of the Privy Chamber in particular.

As it happened, Cromwell's first victory as a faction leader was a relatively easy one. In the aftermath of Wolsey's fall, Henry VIII determined to assume direct control of the government. He was aided by a strange mixture of advisers and favourites: Boleyns, ex-minions, renegade ex-Wolseians like Stephen Gardiner, and the odd great noble like the 3rd Duke of Norfolk. The resulting babel of conflicting counsels combined with Henry's indecisiveness, caution and inefficiency to produce stalemate, the principal sufferers of which were Anne and her followers. For them, therefore, Cromwell came as a godsend. His religious opinions were equally evangelical; his court following was powerful; his grasp of policy acute. The alliance was a natural one: the two factions joined, and for the first time the divorce was pursued with singlemindedness and vigour.

The change showed dramatically in the Parliamentary session of 1532. The 'Reformation' Parliament had been summoned in 1529. It had launched a vigorous attack on a range of clerical 'abuses', particularly ones which touched the pocket of the upper classes; gleefully joined in the hunt against Wolsey, and then, like the government in general, lost both energy and direction. These were recovered in 1532. Parliamentary pressure forced through the Submission of the Clergy, which robbed the English Church of both the will and the capacity to resist Henry; while the conditional Act in Restraint of Annates hit, or rather threatened to hit, Rome where it hurt most, by cutting off papal revenues. It also blocked the most obvious form of retaliation by providing for the appointment and ordination of archbishops and bishops without recourse to the Pope.

Events now moved swiftly to a climax. The ancient Warham, Archbishop of Canterbury, died in August 1532 and Thomas Cranmer, a Boleyn protégé, was appointed. Meanwhile Anne, at last certain of her goal, gave way; became pregnant and was secretly married to Henry on about 25 January 1533. On 3 February Parliament reconvened and rushed through the Act in Restraint of Appeals, which enabled the divorce to be settled finally in England with no possibility of appeal to Rome. The language of the

Act, with its ringing declaration 'that this realm of England is an empire', was magnificent; the reality less so. Cranmer convened his archiepiscopal court in the deliberate obscurity of Dunstable Priory on 10 May, and then, using every procedural device, railroaded through a verdict against Catherine. Francis Bryan played a particularly effective bit part in testifying to the Queen's 'contumacy', or obstinate refusal to recognize the jurisdiction of the court. On 28 May Cranmer pronounced Henry's marriage to Anne valid; and three days later on Whitsunday, 1 June 1533, she was crowned Queen.

She rode from the Tower to Westminster 'in a white litter of white cloth of gold'; and she was dressed all in white and with 'her hair hanging down'. The previous day she had made her entrée into the City, and the City Companies had laid on elaborate pageants to welcome her. The tableau commissioned by the German merchants of the Steelyard, which showed Apollo on Parnassus surrounded by the Muses, was designed by Holbein. Holbein also worked with the King's goldsmith, Cornelys Heyss, to produce a magnificent cradle, decorated with jewels and silverwork and featuring figures of Adam and Eve, executed by Heyss and painted by Holbein. It was a cradle fit for a prince; instead it was a girl, Elizabeth, who was born on 7 September 1533.

The reaction to the Boleyn-Cromwell triumph from the other members of the anti-Wolsey alliance varied. Sir Thomas More, at once the most perceptive and the most pessimistic, resigned as Chancellor the day after the clergy had made their Submission on 15 May 1532. His retirement was less absolute than he pretended and he offered useful advice to the surprisingly vociferous Parliamentary opposition to Henry's proceedings. But it was not his rather limited political activity but the King's hatred, now as deep and unquenchable as his affection had once been, that led to More's imprisonment, trial and execution for treason in 1535. A different case is presented by Stephen Gardiner. A Wolsey protégé, and one of the first to turn against the Cardinal, he had seemed the man most likely to succeed him. Already royal Secretary, he became Bishop of the immensely wealthy see of Winchester in 1531. But he miscalculated badly over the Submission of the Clergy. He led clerical resistance, taking the high line of the liberties of the Church, and was horribly slapped down by Henry. He survived and worked his way back to favour and the leadership of conservatism in the later years of the reign. For the moment, however, he was dished, as were Norfolk and Suffolk in the Council and Carew and Exeter in the Privy Chamber, though it took them longer to realize it. But eventually the fact sunk in: once again nobles and conservatives were the 'out' faction. Only More was out indeed, but the rest now knew that they had destroyed the Cardinal to no purpose.

So it was clear who had lost; it was not yet fully clear, on the other hand, who had gained. It was Cromwell who had given policy its new clarity and urgency; and it was Cromwell who had master-minded the parliamentary strategy of 1532. Nevertheless, there was no question of his succeeding at once to the plenitude of Wolsey's authority. That was made quite sure by the faction structure of the court: on the one hand, he had to share power with an able and intelligent Queen, and on the other both Cromwell and Anne had to face an opposition from the court conservatives that was all the more dangerous for being underground. These shackles on Cromwell, together with the structure of faction which had imposed them, were broken in the second major crisis of faction of 1536.

The roots of this crisis, like those of the first, lay in the King's marital affairs. Henry's second marriage, so long in the making, proved short in happiness. Not only did it fail to produce the longed-for male heir, but also Anne's proud and abrasive character soon became intolerable to her husband. Within a year of the wedding relations had soured and by 1535 the problems were notorious. Immediately the conservatives seized their opportunity. They had long seen that, as Anne had risen, so could she fall. So from the first the fortunes of every 'maiden' who had caught the King's eye were anxiously charted. But not till early 1536 was there the magical combination of circumstance and personality. Then fate put the perfect instrument into their hands: Jane Seymour. She was as different from Anne as could be: demure, quiet, and without an idea in her head. Her motto, which she chose after she became Queen, summarized all: it was 'Bound to obey and serve'. In short, she was the sixteenth century's (and Henry's) ideal woman.

The King and Jane were introduced; Henry was taken and Jane was receptive. But all was not left to nature. Instead, the conservatives in the Privy Chamber, and Sir Nicholas Carew in particular, Henry's intimate of twenty years standing, used their unrivalled knowledge of their master's tastes and character to coach Jane on how to behave. Always the lesson was Anne's own text: that Jane must not 'in any circumstances whatever yield to the King's desire except by the right of marriage'. And she had just enough wit to learn her lesson well. Inflamed by her resistance, Henry sent Jane a purse of sovereigns and a letter. Jane kissed the letter, and returned it to the messenger unopened. Then she threw herself on her knees and addressed the King through his messenger. She begged him to remember that she was a gentlewoman, born of good and honourable parents; that her greatest worldly riches were her honour, which she would not injure for a thousand deaths; and that if he wished to send her money, she prayed that it might be when God had sent him a good marriage. After that well-rehearsed little performance Henry was hers to command.

But before the 'good marriage', to which Jane had so coyly and neatly referred, could take place, Anne had to be got rid of. And the conservatives had an answer for this as well. Their friends, the expert canon lawyers of the Chapel Royal, advised that Anne's marriage could be dissolved and her issue bastardized on the grounds of her previous precontract (that is, binding betrothal) to the Earl of Northumberland. From the same source also came the ruling that was essential to the second string of the conservatives' plot: the restoration of the Princess Mary, Catherine of Aragon's daughter, to the succession from which she had been barred by her parents' divorce. Mary, the canonists argued, had been born '*bona fida parentum*' ('during the good faith of her parents'). This formula nicely squared the circle: it made Mary legitimate, and hence heiress presumptive, without asserting the validity of his first marriage, which Henry found intolerable.

The conservative plot against Anne, now almost certain to be successful, faced Cromwell with a major political challenge – arguably, in fact, the biggest challenge of his career. Carew and his fellows stood for everything the minister most detested: they were committed traditionalists, whose ideal in politics was rule by an aristocratic Council and in religion an equally aristocratic version of Catholic reform. Conversely, Cromwell was, it seemed, indissolubly tied to the Queen both as a political ally and as a radical religious reformer. But, in reality, there were many points of tension between Queen and minister. In particular, they had quarrelled over both the control of patronage and the direction of foreign policy, in which Anne was passionately pro-French while Cromwell inclined judiciously to the Emperor. So Cromwell was happy enough to see Anne fall, provided that one almost impossible condition were met: that the destruction of the Boleyns did not lead to the triumph of the conservatives. There was only one way in which the two events could be separated: Cromwell himself had to take over the plot against Anne.

And that is what he did. First he won the confidence of the three main figures in the conservatives' plot: Carew, the Imperial Ambassador, Eustace Chapuys, whose correspondence supplies us with most of our information about these events, and Mary herself. This alone, bearing in mind his previous relations with the parties, was an astonishing achievement. Next he substituted his own scheme for theirs. Anne was now not to be destroyed by a technicality of canon law, but by an accusation of treason. Her actual crime would be adultery, which in the case of a Queen could be construed as one of the five heads of treasons in the 1351–2 statute, since of course the act contaminated the succession. For Henry, the great advantage of this method was that it killed Anne; the conservatives' proposal, on the other hand, would have left her alive as a vocal and resentful ex-wife – like Catherine of Aragon, from whose troublesome and embarrassing presence the King had just been relieved by her death in January 1536. For Cromwell there were advantages as well: not merely was an adulterous Queen condemned by the act of 1352, so too was the adulterer. This meant that the minister could get rid not only of the Queen but of her followers as well.

The combined pressure on the King of the otherwise implacably opposed forces of Cromwell and the conservatives was irresistible. As usual, however, Henry vacillated to the last moment. Then, on the night of St George's Day, 23 April 1536, the strange processes of his mind arrived at a decision. The next day it was given effect. First, in a blaze of pageantry the King announced that Sir

Nicholas Carew, the Queen's chief antagonist, had been elected a Knight of the Garter in preference to her brother, George, Lord Rochford. The twenty-six Knights of the Order of the Garter, 'the cobrethren and confreres' of the sovereign himself, were the inmost circle of the Tudor élite. To exclude Rochford was an acute public rebuff. That was bad enough for Anne; worse came with the King's other action of 24 April, when, in the profoundest secrecy, he signed a commission instructing Cromwell and a handful of others to investigate certain cases of treason.

A few days were spent in preliminary enquiries. Then the arrests began: on Sunday, 30 April, Mark Smeaton, a favourite musician; on Monday, at the May Day jousts, Anne herself and Henry Norris, the Groom of the Stool; on Tuesday, George, Lord Rochford, Anne's brother; on Wednesday, Sir Francis Weston; on Thursday, William Brereton, and shortly thereafter, Sir Richard Page and the poet Sir Thomas Wyatt. In addition, Sir Francis Bryan was 'suddenly sent for', 'upon his allegiance' to court; subjected to informal interrogation by Cromwell, but escaped actual arrest.

All the accused but Wyatt were members of the King's Privy Chamber and all had been identified more-or-less closely with Anne. But three also had powerful connections with other court parties and these saved them. Wyatt and Page were Cromwell men first and foremost, despite some dalliance – amorous in Wyatt's case, political in Page's – with the Queen. And, no doubt, it was the minister who secured their immunity at an early stage of the investigations, even though they were not released from custody until the affair was over. Certainly, the court conservatives would have been hot against them both because of their religious radicalism, but Cromwell, I suspect, was able to protect them as a *quid pro quo* for not proceeding further with the case against the biggest fish after Lord Rochford to be caught in the net – Sir Francis Bryan. Bryan, as we have seen, had been a prominent early supporter of Anne. However, when the going got rough he had broken with her by a stage-managed quarrel with her brother. Partly he had acted from the prudential motives typical of the 'Vicar of Hell'; but partly because of his genuine religiosity, well expressed in his motto, 'ja tens grace' ('I hope for salvation'). In the early 1530s this religiosity had taken him far back to Rome and wholly back to the bosom of the court conservatives, to whom he was bound by so many ties of common origins and shared experience. Cromwell, as his later actions show, would have been delighted to use Bryan's one-time links with the Boleyns to get so dangerously independent and powerful a courtier out of the way; but equally Bryan was much too valuable a recruit to the conservatives for them to allow him to suffer. Hence the pay-off I have suggested between Bryan, protected by Carew and the rest, and Wyatt and Page, protected by Cromwell.

The other accused, however, had been whole-hearted in their commitment to Anne and for them, as Brereton had said just before his arrest, 'there was no way but one with any matter'. Their fate was sealed and it remained only to fabricate the detailed charges against them. All five were accused of the same offence: adultery with the Queen. In addition, Rochford was accused of incest with his sister and Norris of conspiring the King's death. The basis of these preposterous charges lay in the game of courtly love of which Anne, like any queen, and her own daughter, Elizabeth I, in particular, had been the centre. The tactic adopted by the royal lawyers was to take the ritual for the reality, and to claim that the protestations of devotion, which were the Queen's by right, had been consummated by illicit intercourse, which was treason. Much of the goings-on in Anne's chamber – such as they were – had been discovered by questioning her attendants. Armed with this 'evidence', the Council had confidently thought that it could extract confessions from the accused. In the event, however, and much to everyone's embarrassment, only Smeaton confessed, and that probably under torture. The rest, who were protected by their rank from the means of persuasion used on the unfortunate musician, steadfastly maintained their innocence. But though Anne was resolute under formal examination, she relaxed her guard when she was alone with her maids in the Tower: she racked her memory to discover what incident, what words could have provoked the charges against her. And by a deep irony, these restless speculations, which were immediately reported to Cromwell, provided her enemies with their most useful material.

But even Anne's indiscretions could offer only circumstantial evidence, and that pretty feeble, for the substantive charges. This meant that without the confessions, which in the nature of the act could alone establish the accusations of adultery, the government's case had to rest essentially on sensationalism. This was particularly noticeable in the third count of the indictment, which covered the adulterous incest between Anne and her brother. The crime is ringingly denounced as a contempt of 'all the injunctions of Almighty God and every law of human nature'. But this noble austerity is undercut by the lingeringly salacious details of the alleged act. Even the lovers' passionate kisses are catalogued: some were with open mouth to open mouth; in others, first the sister had put her tongue in her brother's mouth, and then *vice versa*. Well might John Spelman, one of Anne's judges, observe in his notes on the trial that 'all the evidence was bawdy and lechery'.

On such a basis, therefore, was a Queen of England and most of the inner circle of Henry VIII's court destroyed: the four commoners were tried and found guilty on Friday, 12

May; Anne and her brother were condemned the following Monday. On the 17th the men were executed; two days later the Queen herself suffered. From Smeaton's arrest to Anne's death had taken a bare three weeks.

The remaining obstacles to the King's new marriage were cleared just as briskly. On 21 May, two days after Anne's execution, Cranmer declared her marriage to Henry invalid. This made nonsense of the charges of adultery, but at least it bastardized Elizabeth. Then, on 30 May, Jane's 'good marriage' took place. The wedding itself was private, and there was no coronation. But eighteen months later came the crowning blessing indeed with the birth of the longed-for prince on 12 October 1537. It was, as the Marchioness of Dorset wrote to Henry, 'the most joyful news and glad tidings that came to England these many years'. The boy, born on the vigil of St Edward's day, was named after England's royal saint and baptized with the utmost magnificence on 15 October. On 18 October Queen Jane's eldest brother Edward was made Earl of Hereford, and her brother Thomas knighted. (Her other brother Henry had also come to court, but quickly left to return home; cultivate his garden and die, long after, in his bed.) Their sister, however, had not recovered from a difficult birth. On 23 October the royal doctors, headed by Dr Butts, reported that she had had 'a natural lax' and seemed to improve; then in the evening her condition suddenly worsened. The following morning her confessor shrived her and administered extreme unction. Within a few hours she was dead.

The subsequent strident Protestantism of both her family and her son have led to much confusion about Jane. At the time, as her good Catholic ending would suggest, she had no truck with such notions. Rather the contrary: she had been a candidate of the conservative party and had been coached by Carew. And he had not limited his lessons to the art of seducing Henry, but had given them a more directly political slant as well. Once again Jane was receptive. In public she showed the utmost deference and respect to the Princess Mary; and in private, Chapuys reported, she furthered the conservatives' cause by beseeching Henry to restore Mary to the succession. The King roundly told her that she was a fool and ought to be suing for the advancement of the children that they would have together and no other. To which she replied that

> *in asking for the restoration of the Princess she conceived she was seeking the rest and tranquillity of the King, herself, her future children, and the whole realm; for without that neither your majesty (i.e. the Emperor) nor his people would ever be content.*

Which sounds like another testimony to Carew's abilities as a speech writer and to Jane's well-trained memory.

Cromwell of course had not destroyed Anne to replace her with another political Queen, still less with one who was the mouthpiece of conservative reaction. Now the mask came off. Having used the conservatives to destroy Anne and her friends, he now turned on his erstwhile allies. They suddenly found themselves accused of working to restore Mary to the succession, which of course they had done – and so too had Cromwell claimed to be doing. But such an attempt, despite the rupture of the Boleyn marriage, remained treasonable. The Princess herself was told that, unless she did what hitherto she had steadfastly refused to do and recognized formally the dissolution of her mother's marriage and her own bastardy, her friends were lost. Under intense pressure, both from her English adherents and from Chapuys, she capitulated. The lives of the conservative factions were saved, but their influence was broken. And moreover, their fate had only been delayed: two years later, in the course of 1538–9, Cromwell succeeded in planting charges of treason on the most important members of the group – the Marquess of Exeter, Sir Edward Neville and Sir Nicholas Carew himself. All were executed. At almost the same time, the minister contrived to bring two other leading Gentlemen of the Privy Chamber, Sir Anthony Browne and Sir Francis Bryan, who were closely tied to the conservatives, into acute disfavour with the King. So much so, in fact, that Bryan, whose highly-strung temperament had stood up remarkably well to Cromwell's abortive attack of 1536, now almost died under the nervous strain.

The events of 1536–9, by their horror and heartlessness, raise the problem of royal manipulation in its most extreme form. The means used to ruin Anne are transparent, but how Henry was brought to destroy his intimates of twenty years standing, like Norris and Carew, remains ultimately mysterious. I would guess, however, that Cromwell deliberately put them in a situation where they had to reveal that they regarded some other duty as highly as their allegiance to the King. Norris refused – even when questioned by Henry himself – to accuse Anne Boleyn: therefore he valued the King's wife above the King; Carew always worked for Mary: therefore he valued the King's daughter above the King. And as the case of Sir Thomas More shows, the unveiling of such a double loyalty could be guaranteed to turn the King's deepest affection into implacable hatred.

But if the techniques used remain doubtful, their consequences do not. For though the second crisis of faction of Henry VIII's reign resembled the first formally, in that two of the court factions again united against the third, its outcome was totally different. The first crisis had only one victim, and he – Wolsey – anticipated possible execution by an opportune natural death; it realigned the court factions but destroyed none of them, and it led to a period of multi-faction rule. The second crisis, in contrast, slaughtered two thirds of the inner court; it rooted out one court faction completely (the Boleyns) and decimated another (the conservatives), and secured Cromwell a complete and unprecedented dominance over both court and government. The difference was due, above all, to Cromwell's ruthless employment of the axe and to his single-mindedness as a faction leader.

The latter meant also that there was no question of his using the great emptying of the Privy Chamber in these three years to neutralize the court, as Wolsey had done after the administrative purge of 1526. Instead he packed the vacant places with his own loyal adherents: Ralph Sadler, Philip Hoby, Peter Mewtis, Anthony Denny and the rest. But these men were not only the minister's followers, they were also convinced, articulate and, generally, educated evangelicals, perhaps even Protestants. Moreover when, like Denny who succeeded his first master Sir Francis Bryan as Chief Gentleman of the Privy Chamber on the latter's fall from favour in 1538, they found themselves in a position to exercise patronage themselves, they appointed similarly hot radicals to the places in their gift. By the late 1530s, therefore, the religious complexion of the inner court was overwhelmingly evangelical.

Just as dramatic was the social change. The men whom Cromwell had executed or driven into political death were courtiers born; the men he put in their place would in more ordinary times have made their careers as merchants, lawyers or dons. Never in a thousand years would a Sadler, for instance, have become a courtier if the all-powerful Cromwell had not made him one. Only once did Henry object to these strange recruits. The minister had tried to appoint the donnish propagandist Richard Moryson to Privy Chamber office. Moryson was, I guess, a tedious prig; at any rate Henry drew the line and the appointment, though gazetted, took no effect. 'I blush as long as I am at the court', Moryson confided to his patron. Stung perhaps by these complaints of a good servant; more likely disturbed by the rebuff to his own power, Cromwell tried again and this time successfully foisted Moryson on the reluctant King. But the most unlikely recruit was not the minister's servant but the minister himself. In 1539 Cromwell assumed the titular headship of the Privy Chamber; then concurrently in 1540 took the office of Lord Great Chamberlain of England. The bureaucrat minister had become the King's chief body servant.

All of which helps to explain why, in the winter of 1539–40, Cromwell felt able to force, not a body servant into the Privy Chamber, but a wife into the King's bed. Henry had long recovered from the death of Jane Seymour and needed a wife. Various Hapsburg and Valois princesses were tried without success. Which left the way open to a dynastic second-best like a lady of the House of Cleves, a strategically important dukedom between the Low Countries and the German Empire. A Cleves marriage suited Cromwell's foreign and religious policies well enough, and Henry found Holbein's portrait of Anne, one of the Duke's two sisters, appealing. Ambassadors' reports fed the fire and a treaty was signed.

But Henry's first glimpse of Anne, stolen ahead of the arranged meeting at Greenwich, was a disaster. The King made his distaste plain and desperately tried to wriggle out of the marriage. But Cromwell held his nose to the grindstone. The last-minute legal obstacles that Henry had thrown up were brushed aside and the wedding was solemnized on 6 January 1540, only three days later than planned. At the same time Cromwell set Denny, his ablest partisan in the Privy Chamber, to work. Denny 'took evermore occasion to praise [the Queen] to the King's highness'. Denny could do most things with the King, but here at least the power of influence failed. Wearied at last by his importunity, Henry told Denny: 'How he would utter plainly to him, as to a servant whom he used secretly about him . . . that he could never . . . be provoked and stirred to know her carnally.' Swallow Moryson Henry must; endure Anne finally he would not. Cromwell, who had tied the knot, now had to undo it. It was a tight corner, but with his extraordinary skill at political manoeuvre he might well have been able to fight his way out of it.

That he did not was due above all to his failure fully to control the other power centre of Tudor England, the Council. He had enemies there, like the Duke of Norfolk, and Stephen Gardiner, the able and ambitious Bishop of Winchester, that he had never removed. Why is something of a mystery. But probably it was because he saw the court as a more immediate threat. By 1539–40 that threat was eliminated and Cromwell was at leisure to turn to the Council. That gave, it may be conjectured, Norfolk and Gardiner the courage of desperation. The fiasco of the Cleves marriage, which Cromwell had engineered, played into their hands, and they struck home by accusing the minister of the sacramentarian heresy, or denial of the real presence. The charge, with its overtones of anabaptism and anarchy, temporarily overbalanced Henry and Cromwell took the road of so many of his opponents to the block.

7

THE LAST YEARS

The Rule of Faction

CROMWELL, ARCHITECT of the Reformation and arch-politician of faction, was not replaced. Instead Henry, for the first time since the earliest years of the reign, ruled alone, without a single principal adviser (for even in the 'inter-ministerium' between Wolsey and Cromwell, Anne Boleyn, despite her sex, fulfilled much of the role of chief councillor). But the Henry of the 1540s was very different from the prince charming of 1509. The physical change can be measured with precision from Henry's various suits of armour. He was 6 foot 2 inches tall: in about 1512 he was a trim 32 inches round the waist, by about 1520 he had filled out to 35 inches and by 1545 was a gross 54 inches.

The alteration showed even more in the face. Contemporaries had waxed lyrical about his youthful beauty, and indeed his early portraits show a broad, fair countenance. The tiny eyes, set deep and rather close together, and the small, prissily-pursed mouth strike a note of doubt, but over all it is pleasant enough. By 1544, however, this had turned into the appalling mask shown in Cornelys Matsys's portrait. The forehead has been exaggerated by total baldness into a vast dome; the cheeks sag pendulous with fat; and in this smooth landscape eyes and mouth appear as minute slits. Egg-shaped, it is a Humpty-

Dumpty of nightmare. When, half a century and another dynasty later, Sir Walter Raleigh wrote of Henry VIII that 'if all the pictures and patterns of a merciless prince were lost in the world, they might all again be painted to the life out of the story of this king', he was using the word 'picture' as a metaphor. But in Matsys's portrait of Henry there is the actual image of tyranny in all its nastiness.

The degeneration of character was just as marked. Gone was the rather appealing diffidence and naivety of the first years, to be replaced not by quiet self-confidence but by bombast and bragging. 'It is I', he is alleged to have said to Secretary Petre, 'that made both Cromwell, Wriothesley and Paget good Secretaries, and so I must do to thee.' The conceit of the statement is exceeded only by its untruthfulness. But then truth was a prime victim of these years as Henry's suspiciousness, first stimulated by Wolsey, turned into a huge distorting glass through which he viewed the world. It could turn the most trivial incident into a conspiracy; the lightest word into treason.

No doubt age had a major part in all this. But so did the King's fifth marriage. Obviously anyone who marries six times does so out of hope rather than experience. But most of Henry's marital disasters touched him but little. When Catherine of Aragon died in January 1536 Henry wore 'yellow for mourning'; and a few months later, on the break-up of his second marriage, he flaunted Anne Boleyn's alleged promiscuity. 'He believed more than a hundred had had to do with her', he said and claimed to have written a 'tragedy' about it. 'You never', observed Chapuys, 'saw prince nor man who made greater show of his horns, or bore them more pleasantly.' Similarly, the dissolution of his marriage with Anne of Cleves on grounds of non-consummation was brushed off. His lack of appetite was blamed only on the 'loathsomeness' of her body; after all, had he not, as he told his physician Dr

Butts, meanwhile had 'two wet dreams' (*duas pollutiones nocturnas in somno*)? Once again Henry was divorced but not downcast.

Rather the contrary in fact, for in the offing was Catherine Howard. Anne of Cleves had been Cromwell's candidate; Catherine was put forward by his enemies. She was niece of the Duke of Norfolk and the King was first introduced to her while he was staying with Bishop Gardiner. The Bishop, indeed, probably played go-between; if he did, he had a good eye for the ladies. Catherine was young and flirtatious and Henry fell in love at first sight. She became his mistress immediately; soon it was clear she would become Queen. Rumour had it she was pregnant by him when Anne of Cleves was finally divorced on 9 July 1540; three weeks later they were married, and by the beginning of August she was acknowledged as Queen.

It was a true case of Winter, or at least late Autumn, marrying Spring. Winter was intoxicated, rejuvenated; Spring was bored out of her sweet but empty little head. For Henry was not of course the first or the most attractive of lovers. Her father, Lord Edmund Howard, though the younger son of a duke, was wretchedly poor and Catherine had been brought up in the household of her step-grandmother, the Dowager Duchess of Norfolk. There she seems to have been free to do as the fancy took her. And the fancy took her pretty often. First there was a musician, Henry Mannock, and then a gentleman of the household called Francis Dereham. That affair indeed became an actual if unacknowledged betrothal. But it was broken off when she was summoned at court. Dereham was no longer grand enough; and in any case her eye had lit on her attractive young cousin, Thomas Culpepper, Henry's current favourite among the Gentlemen of the Privy Chamber.

There things stood when she was thrust forward, first as royal mistress and then as Queen. Neither the greatness nor the danger of the position seems to have made the least impression on her and soon it was business as before. She summoned Culpepper and told him 'if I had tarried still in the maiden's chamber I would have tried you'. Whether she subsequently did or not must remain a matter of speculation. Culpepper denied it, but their behaviour gave him the lie. Aided and abetted by Lady Rochford, a Lady of the Queen's Privy Chamber, they spent hours at a time alone together. The Queen herself would 'in every house seek for the backdoors and backstairs herself'; once, if the indictment is to be believed, they even kept tryst in her stool chamber ('a secret and vile place' as the Act of Attainder put it).

Catherine in short was doing what Anne Boleyn was supposed to have done. She was promiscuous; her principal lover was a Gentleman of the Privy Chamber; and there was even a continuity of personnel since Lady Rochford was the widow of Anne's brother George Boleyn, Lord Rochford. Finally her fall, which came faster than Anne's, was dramatic in timing and triggered by faction.

On 30 October 1541 the court returned to Hampton Court after an unusually long and distant progress to the north. Next day was All Saints' Day. The King was in an excellent mood, relaxed by his holiday and rejoicing in his new marriage. Very properly he took advantage of the high festival to give thanks to God. Safe at last 'after sundry troubles of mind which had happened to him by marriages', he offered up prayers 'for the good life he led and trusted to lead' with Catherine. His confessor, Longland, Bishop of Lincoln, was commanded publicly to 'make like prayer and give like thanks with him'. The King prayed too soon. At mass the following day, Cranmer, the

Archbishop of Canterbury, handed the King a paper which he begged him to read in the strictest privacy. In the paper were full and documented details of his Queen's affairs.

Cranmer's motives are not in doubt. He was through-and-through evangelical and, as such, a leading opponent of the Howards. And he had worked with others of the same stamp. He had consulted with another Howard enemy, Edward Seymour, Queen Jane's brother and Earl of Hertford; while the information he gave Henry was supplied by John Lascelles, who was to go to the stake as a Protestant martyr in 1546. All three were playing, though on the opposite side, the same game of politico-religious faction as Carew and his friends had been when they had traduced Anne in 1536.

But with the King's reactions the parallel breaks down. In 1536 Henry had grasped eagerly at the 'revelation' of Anne's adultery. In 1541 he first flatly refused to believe the accusations against Catherine; then, when they were proved beyond doubt, he collapsed. Tears flowed, 'which was strange in his courage'. The sequel was different too. In 1536 the net was cast ever wider, until a whole court faction was destroyed. In 1541, on the other hand, there were only four deaths: Culpepper and Dereham were executed on 10 December; Catherine and Lady Rochford a few months later in February 1542. On Sunday, the 12th, Catherine was told that she was to be beheaded on the Monday. She asked to be shown the block; went through a form of rehearsal, and the following day 'made the most godly and Christian end'. She had learned to behave like a Queen at last.

Many others of course had been implicated – so many indeed that the ordinary prisons could not hold them all and the royal lodgings had to be used as an overflow. In the event, however, all, even those most closely linked to the Queen, escaped lightly. Her brother Charles was merely expelled from the King's Privy Chamber; her uncle Lord William Howard and her conniving grandmother, the Dowager Duchess, were indeed condemned for misprision of treason, for which the penalties – perpetual imprisonment and forfeiture of all property – were anything but light. But both were released and pardoned after a few months. And the really big fish, Norfolk and Gardiner, were not touched at all. Why so light a toll? Partly because there was no single, ruthless intelligence, like Cromwell's, to exploit the situation; and partly because of the peculiar balance of power which had followed Cromwell's fall.

His enemies, Norfolk and Gardiner, had had their power base in the King's Council, and with the minister's removal they consolidated their hold. The fact was expressed institutionally. On 10 August 1540 the Council, which had led such a protean existence in the reign, was set up on a more formal basis. It was given its own clerk and minute book; had a small fixed personnel of about nineteen; and met more-or-less daily, usually at court. The Council had become the Privy Council. Recently it has been fashionable to see the change as a piece of administrative business left over, as it were, from Cromwell's reforming regime. There is some truth in this, but more important was another influence, that of the nobility.

The nobility had a clear concept of good government. This should consist of a small, ruling council, dominated by themselves. Whenever they emerged into the limelight, such a Council runs affairs. This happened in the reaction after Henry VII's death; after the fall of Wolsey; and in the crisis of 1536, which began with the fall of Anne Boleyn and ended with the petering out of the rebellion in the north known as the Pilgrimage of Grace. So it was in 1540. The men who destroyed Cromwell were essentially an aristocratic party, led by the premier duke, Norfolk, and the richest prelate, Gardiner. Their bias showed very early in the charges levelled against Cromwell. These began with a sneering reference to the 'very base and low degree' from which the King had raised him, and ended by accusing him of holding the nobility 'in great disdain'; had he not threatened, 'if the lords would handle him so, that he would give them such a breakfast as never was made in England, and that the proudest of them should know?'

In the event, the lords served breakfast first; got rid of Cromwell and imposed their own upper-crust vision of politics. Its centrepiece was the new Privy Council. The Privy Council, unlike the old Council, was made up almost exclusively of office-holders. This does not mean, as the administrative historians have it, that it was a proto-cabinet of the heads of bureaucratic departments. There were such people in the Privy Council, like the Chancellors of the Courts of Augmentations and First Fruits and Tenths, but they were its lowest-ranking members. Weightier far in both numbers and prestige were the holders of those very different entities, the 'greatest offices of the realm'. These offices had two distinct lineages. Some – like the Great Chamberlaincy or the Earl Marshalship – were the ancient household and military offices of the Anglo-Norman kings. Others – like the offices of Lord Chancellor or Lord Privy Seal – were the senior administrative positions of the later medieval monarchy. The former were the core of the noble Great Council that developed into the Upper House of Parliament; the latter were the backbone of the King's actual working Council of advisers.

But by the mid sixteenth century the distinctions between the two groups of offices were eroding. The first were no longer hereditary noble appanages; the second were no longer the preserve of the clergy. And almost all had seen their original functions either vanish or go into abeyance: the Lord Admiral no longer commanded ships;

the Lord President of the Council hardly ever presided; even the Lord Treasurer had nothing particularly to do with money. Only the shell of antiquity and prestige survived. The time was ripe for rationalization.

This is what was achieved in 1539–40. The Act of Precedence of 1539 fused all the 'great offices' into a single table of rank; while the conciliar reform of 1540 made them all members of the new Privy Council. The result was a novel and idiosyncratic form of Council, that had little in common save the name with the less noble and more 'expert' Privy Council of Elizabeth I. Instead the mid Tudor Privy Council consisted largely of prestigious ministers-without-portfolio who held offices and pursued new ones, not for what they did but for where they put them in the political pecking order. It was a peculiarly aristocratic view of counsel for a Council that was to be predominantly aristocratic.

Just how aristocratic is only just being realized. The Act of 1539 listed eleven great offices. Of these, the six originally military and household offices of Great Chamberlain, Constable, Earl Marshal, Lord Admiral, Lord Great Master of the Household, and Lord Chamberlain of the Household could only be held by a peer. While of the other five sometime bureaucratic posts of Lord Chancellor, Lord Treasurer, Lord President of the Council, Lord Privy Seal and Principal Secretary, the first four in practice always went to a noble, leaving only the Secretaryship, which was much the least important in rank, to be held by a commoner. The result (allowing for pluralism on the one hand and nobles who were councillors without being office holders on the other) was that peers and prelates made up 58 per cent of the Privy Council in 1540, 48 per cent in 1547, 61 per cent in 1551 and 57 per cent in 1558.

But if the peerage now dominated the Council, so in a

sense had the Council taken over the peerage. The figures alone are striking. With a lay peerage of about forty, almost a quarter were now councillors; and at the magnate level of earl and above the proportion rises even higher to five out of fifteen, or a full third. And numbers do not tell the whole story. Traditionally precedence among the peers was determined by two things: by rank within the peerage, so that an earl outranked a baron, a marquess an earl, and so on; and within each rank by date of creation, with the oldest title ranking highest. The Act of 1539 changed all that. Rank now also depended on conciliar office, and the new system overlaid the old.

The results show dramatically in the attendance register for the first session of the House of Lords under the new rules. William Fitzwilliam, the Earl of Southampton, rose from his position as second to last of the earls, which he was by date of creation (1537), to second from the top, which he was by virtue of his office of Lord Admiral. While the Earl of Arundel, already fifteenth of his line and with his title going back to 1140, saw himself fall, because he held no office, from first to third, behind the upstart Fitzwilliam. So what? Indeed the most recent historian of the House of Lords says lightly that the effects of the Act were 'very limited'. He views it, however, from the happy egalitarianism of antipodean society, where 'precedence', I imagine, is thought to be a four-wheel-drive Honda. The Tudors saw things differently. And Arundel's son redeemed the disgrace to his house by going determinedly for the conciliar office that would restore it to its proper position.

Others did likewise. The result was a marked politic-ization of the peerage. The Tudor 'service nobility' (not one of the peers in the Privy Council of 1540 had a title older than Henry's own reign) had always seen the court as their natural forum of action. And only the jealousy of

Wolsey and Cromwell had kept them away. But even the few families of ancient lineage now had, thanks to the new rules of precedence, real incentive for political involvement. And overwhelmingly these new or newish recruits to central politics were conservative: socially, politically, religiously. The fact can hardly have surprised Norfolk and his cronies; indeed they had probably banked on it from the start.

But not only did the creation of the Privy Council reinforce in depth the conservatives' power over the Council, the Howard marriage bid fair to give them control of the court as well. The Queen's brother Charles, as usual, was put into the King's Privy Chamber; her uncle, Lord William Howard, was already a member of it; while Robert, Earl of Sussex and Norfolk's side-kick, succeeded Cromwell as Lord Great Chamberlain and effective head of the whole upper household. But the debacle of Catherine's fall put paid to all that. Instead the court, and the Privy Chamber above all, remained essentially as Cromwell had left it, as the preserve of his own radical appointees.

The most important of these was Anthony Denny. Born in 1501, he was the son of a leading lawyer-administrator of the Exchequer. His upbringing contained elements of old and new. He received a fashionable humanist education, first at St Paul's where he was taught by the great grammarian Lely, and subsequently at St John's College, Cambridge. But then he went on to an old-style 'household' apprenticeship as servant to Sir Francis Bryan, whose household was in its way as much a seminary for the rising generation as Cambridge. Denny was already astute enough to benefit from the downs as well as the ups of his master's vertiginous career. When Bryan became Chief Gentleman of the Privy Chamber in 1536, Denny, carried on his coat tails, was appointed a Groom; equally, when

Bryan fell from favour in the winter of 1538–9, Denny succeeded him as Chief Gentleman. As such he emerged as the courtier *par excellence* of the last years of the reign.

His rise demonstrates how much things had changed. He had none of the minions' animal high spirits or athleticism. Instead there was a high-Victorian seriousness about him (not unmixed with high-Victorian hypocrisy), and a fondness for learning that verged on the bookish. All this made sense in the light of the alterations in Henry himself. *Gravitas* had come with corpulence. He had stopped jousting; hunted only intermittently, and spent more and more time with books. An illumination in his Book of Psalms (*c.*1545) shows him reading in his Bedchamber; while pencil annotations in his own hand in the margin take us with a rather touching directness into his mind. Verse 25 of Psalm 37 reads: 'I have been young, and now am old; yet I have not seen the righteous forsaken, nor his seed begging bread.' Besides this Henry wrote: 'a painful saying' (*dolens dictum*). For moods like this Denny, with his 'sincere affection to God and his holy word', was an ideal companion.

Some things about the courtier of course changed less. Denny was as charming as Norris, and even won the same sobriquet of 'gentle'. And he had the same infinite capacity for taking pains. Even a tiresome suitor like Nicholas Wentworth would find him willing not only to lend an ear but also to help prepare his suit in writing, 'which, considering his attendance upon the King and other business is very much for him to do'. It was. But it was activity with a purpose. A patron who takes pains wins clients. And Denny wanted clients. It was the same with his patronage of learning. Figures as diverse as Thomas Elyot of the older generation, or Roger Ascham of the new, benefited, so that by 1546 Thomas Langley, printer to the Prince of Wales, could hail Denny as 'a favourable supporter of all good learning and a very *Maecenas* of all towards wits'. No doubt Denny's 'desire of knowledge of antiquities' counted; so too did his awareness that grateful scholars would make the 'tuneful court' echo with 'resonant hymns' of praise to his 'universal popularity'.

This element of calculation, of 'taking thought for the morrow' (he had obviously read the Sermon on the Mount less thoroughly than Henry had done the Psalms), made him the most politically successful holder of the Privy Chamber office in the reign. Here once again the man matched the moment. In these last years Henry himself was more politically active than ever before. He took more decisions and devoted more time to business. To have an acutely political intelligence like Denny's on call twenty-four hours a day was invaluable. Denny acted in two main capacities. First, he was an informal adviser with whom the King would mull over state business after he had discussed it with his Secretary. And second, and still more important, he was head of a private royal administrative machine.

Even at his most careless, Henry had never entirely ceased to involve himself in administration. He was in personal charge of the cash reserves or 'privy coffers'; while his signature or 'sign manual' remained the prime motor of government. A minister like Cromwell had made heavy inroads into these activities (for reasons, it should be added, that were purely political and owed nothing to any notion of 'bureaucratic' development). But with Cromwell's removal Henry's administrative involvement, like his political, rose. There was in any case more to do. The plunder of the monasteries meant that there was more money to keep and more lands and offices to bestow. Monastic spoil also helped make possible renewed war against France in 1544, and war always brought the King to the fore governmentally. In all this Denny was Henry's chief assistant. He ran the royal deposit account as Keeper of Whitehall Palace (£250,000 passed through his hands in 1540–4) and he organized the signing of documents.

So heavy indeed did his duties become that he set up his own staff. His office manager was his brother-in-law John Gates, who was also a Gentleman of the Privy Chamber. Gates was the perfect complement to Denny. Denny could deploy his charm at the front of the shop while Gates did the dirty work at the back (Gates was to employ the same talents on a wider stage when he became chief hatchet man to the Duke of Northumberland in the next reign). Under Gates's general supervision were specialist clerks: Nicholas Bristow was the accountant of the Privy coffers; while William Clerk dealt with the sign manual.

The latter was put on a new footing in 1545. The King had always hated the business of signing and would put it off on any and every excuse. Finally he gave it up altogether. A crude wooden stamp (the 'wet stamp') had regularly been used to authenticate circulars and the like; now the system was extended. A new stamp – the 'dry stamp' – was made. The stamp, as its name implies, was applied uninked to the paper, probably with the aid of a small screw press. It left a light and accurate impression of the King's signature, which was gone over in ink by Clerk (a highly skilled calligrapher) to produce a near-perfect facsimile of the sign manual. And the stamp was used, not only for circulars, but for every document that the King would normally have signed. At first Henry, understandably, kept the stamp himself and Denny and Gates only acted as witnesses when Clerk applied it. But soon Henry handed over the stamp in its 'little coffer of black leather' to Gates's custody. He had alienated his signature as completely as earlier Kings had alienated their seals to their Chancellors.

The result of all this was that in the last years of the reign Henry was exposed to the pull of equal and opposite

112

forces: a revitalized and conservative Privy Council on the one hand, and, on the other, a radical Privy Chamber that was ruled by Gates's iron hand inside Denny's velvet glove. Conflict between court and Council had been endemic; now it burst into the open in a series of sensational but inconclusive plots.

The sequence had begun early in 1540. As Cromwell fought desperately for survival, he had a conservative peer, Arthur Plantagenet, Viscount Lisle and Deputy of Calais, and a conservative prelate, Sampson, Bishop of Chichester and Dean of the Chapel Royal, arrested for treason. His own death saved them from the same fate and the conservatives pressed their advantage home. All Cromwell's leading servants found themselves under investigation and in January 1541 Sir Thomas Wyatt and Sir Ralph Sadler were arrested and led to the Tower, with hands tightly bound and under a heavy guard of twenty-four armed men. Wyatt had been flamboyant about both his loyalty to Cromwell and his Lutheranism; Sadler was more circumspect, but the bigger catch. Early in 1540 the Secretaryship had been divided between two of Cromwell's servants: Thomas Wriothesley who acted as Secretary to the Council; and Sadler who was Secretary to the King in the Privy Chamber. To remove him would be a conservative triumph. But it proved elusive. For two days after the arrest of Sadler on 16 January 1541, Sir John Wallop, a Gentleman of the Privy Chamber of quite the opposite religious and political inclination, was recalled as Ambassador to France and immediately arrested for treason on his return. It was stalemate, and everybody – 'right' and 'left' – escaped after the usual round of confession and submission.

Two years later there was an even more violent oscillation. In spring 1543 Cranmer himself was accused of heresy by his own cathedral clergy, orchestrated from the wings by Gardiner. Henry, however, treated the accusation lightly, telling Cranmer, 'I know now who is the greatest heretic in Kent', and appointing him to investigate the charges himself! Foiled of the Archbishop, who enjoyed something of a charmed life, the conservatives struck even nearer the King. They had 'uncovered a nest of heretics' among the musical establishment of the Chapel Royal at Windsor and among minor members of the royal household there. And from such small fry the trail led straight to the radicals of the Privy Chamber. But at the moment the affair broke, the King, to everyone's astonishment, married again. The lady was Catherine Parr. She was young, twice widowed, short of stature, and, so the French Ambassador thought, even less attractive than Anne of Cleves. But above all she inclined clearly to the 'new' in religion. Two months later pardons were granted to all the members of the Privy Chamber under suspicion in the Windsor affair.

What are we to make of all this?

There are two main schools of interpretation. One sees the King as puppet-master, making and unmaking (though not wholly undoing) his ministers to demonstrate his absolute power. The other views Henry not as the master but as the creature of factions, which pull him first one way and then the other in a struggle that he may not fully have understood and that he certainly never fully controlled. Logically the two positions are contradictory. Actually they may both be true. The King probably thought (after all, he had good reason to) that he was in charge; his ministers and courtiers equally seem to have thought and behaved as though they could manipulate the King. Perspective is all.

But a different sort of perspective, namely the politics of the whole reign, offers a different and less ambiguous answer. There was in fact no novelty in the outstanding features of Henry's behaviour in the 1540s – like his

19. Henry VIII writing in his own hand to Wolsey in *c*. 1519 about a feared noble conspiracy. Since, as the letter says, Henry found writing 'somewhat tedious and painful', he reserved it for major business.

20. The Field of Cloth of Gold, 1520. The meeting between Henry VIII and Francis I was the centre-piece of the diplomatic flurry of these years which kept Wolsey's enemies busy away from court.

21. The Battle of Pavia, 1525, in which Francis I was defeated and captured by Charles V's generals, transformed foreign affairs. England allied with France; while Charles took control of the Pope and stopped him granting Henry's divorce.

22. Although the inscription on this Holbein drawing has long been rejected, the laced-up dress and heavy, almost swollen, jaw-line correspond closely to contemporary descriptions of Anne Boleyn.

23. Thomas Cranmer, Archbishop of Canterbury 1532-55. Promoted by the Boleyns, he survived their fall to become the leader of the 'new' religion. He had many enemies, but Henry VIII always saved him.

24. Holbein's drawing of Sir John Russell, later Earl of Bedford. Of humble origins, he was promoted to the Privy Chamber by Wolsey and went on to found one of the greatest noble families.

25. Holbein's portrait of Thomas Cromwell, chief minister 1532-40. A superb administrator and politician, his radical social and religious policies were loved or loathed. Accused of heresy, he was executed in 1540.

26. Stephen Gardiner, Bishop of Winchester, the brains behind political and religious conservatism in the later part of the reign. An overbearing and brilliant lawyer, he was finally outsmarted in the manoeuvres over Henry's will.

27. Procession of Knights of the Garter in heraldic surcoats, 1534. The twenty-six knights, 'cobreathren and confreres' of the King, met at Windsor on St George's day to feast and fill in vacancies.

28. Sir William Butts, Henry's chief physician till his death in 1545. A religious radical, he used his excellent bedside manner to promote and protect bright young men from Cambridge.

29. Sir Anthony Browne, as one of the King's young minions. Later Cromwell denounced him as 'a vain old beau', but he survived to become an important conservative leader in the 1540s.

30. Sir Anthony Denny, head of the Privy Chamber. A 'favourer of good learning', his control of the private apartments made him the key figure in the struggles over Henry's death-bed.

31. Henry VIII reading in his Bedchamber, from an illustration in his Psalter. Ageing, he spent more time with books, and in the margin of this one are his pencilled notes written in often gloomy mood.

32. Perhaps Catherine Parr, Henry's last Queen. A blue-stocking and religious radical, her chamber became the scene of passionate debate among the preachers and young hot-heads of the court.

33., 34. Holbein's drawings of Sir Philip and La Hoby. They were two of the leading courtiers who were accused of heresy at Windsor in 154 but later pardoned.

35. A seventeenth-century woodcut of the burning of Ann Ascue in 1546. Great court ladies succoured her in prison, but she protected them by her silence under torture.

36. Henry Howard, Earl of Surrey, extravagantly dressed as an Italian princeling and surrounded by the sort of heraldic display that gave his enemies an excuse for destroying him in December 1546.

37. Holbein's portrait of Anne of Cleves. Sketched hastily on parchment from the life, and subsequently mounted and painted over, this artful portrait helped persuade Henry into his disastrous fourth marriage.

38. Sir William Paget, the King's Secretary and 'master of practices'. He put together the coalition of Denny and the Seymours that defeated the Howards in the power struggle over Henry's death-bed.

39. The last page of Henry VIII's will, signed with the stamp of Henry's signature and antedated. The doctored document paved the way for Edward Seymour, Prince Edward's uncle, to take over power.

40. Henry's death-bed as the victorious party wanted it to be seen. Above Henry gives power to Edward supported by Seymour; below the Pope is overthrown, while the conservative councillors look on.

tendency to postpone decisions till the last possible moment and then take them in a rush, often late at night; or his fondness for secret messages, rings, tokens, and the whole apparatus of cloak-and-dagger. They are present throughout the reign and reveal themselves particularly clearly in those earlier crises of faction: the fall of Wolsey and the Boleyn affair of 1536. The difference lay not so much in Henry as in circumstance. In the earlier crises overwhelming pressure finally forced a decision out of him. In the 1540s, on the other hand, the pressures on him were so finely balanced that his natural indecisiveness was never overcome. Instead the pans of the scale trembled but never swung; and while intended victims went often enough to the Tower, they rarely proceeded to the block.

And they were usually quite clear about why they had escaped. While in public they might thank the King's mercy or the Queen's gracious intervention, in private they told gleefully how their friends had outwitted their enemies. Particularly crucial in this game was the role of members of the Privy Chamber. They, as it were, could reach the parts that others could not. They alone attended the King at those odd times and places when he was increasingly likely to make up his mind or – just as important – change it. For instance, in 1544 Cranmer's secretary Ralph Morice wrote to Denny and Dr William Butts, the King's physician, to ask them to protect his radical curate, Richard Turner. Cranmer was too worried about his own position to do anything, but perhaps they could help? Butts waited until a suitable moment, then, 'spying a time when the King was in trimming and washing', he 'pleasantly and merrily beginneth to insinuate unto the King the effect of the matter'. The result was that Henry stood his earlier decision on its head, and 'whereas before he [had] commanded the said Turner to be whipped out of the country, he now commanded him to be retained as a faithful subject'.

The same machinery could, of course, be used in the opposite direction. For though Denny and his party were the dominant group in the Privy Chamber, Gardiner was by no means friendless there. And the fact saved him. In 1544 his nephew, Germayne Gardiner, turned Catholic traitor. Gardiner himself kept his hands less clean than he should, and, according to Foxe, Henry was brought to agree that he should be investigated for treason too. Typically the decision was taken in the evening between the King and the Duke of Suffolk. 'Howbeit', the Duke is reported as saying, 'our talk was not so secret, but that some of his friends of the Privy Chamber, . . . suspecting the matter, sent him word thereof.' Gardiner hastened to the court early the following morning, made confession and won pardon. But on balance the Privy Chamber worked to thwart Gardiner, not to protect him.

And it was this fact which shipwrecked the conservative reaction of the 1540s. In 1539–40 everything seemed to be going their way. They had outlawed religious dissent; destroyed the principal architect of the Reformation, and enjoyed a clear majority in the ruling Privy Council. Only the Privy Chamber stood between them and victory. But it was enough. Protected themselves by the King's special favour, the members of the Privy Chamber were able to extend that protection to others. The result was that, though Gardiner managed to send to the stake a few clergy who preached too loudly, nobody who mattered suffered the same fate. The nearest squeak was had by the young 'Protestant' poet-master, George Blage, who was a frequenter though not a member of the Privy Chamber. He was arrested, tried and sentenced within a mere three days. But the Privy Chamber once more protected its own. They petitioned the King in a body and secured his pardon and return to the court. On his first visit there after his rehabilitation, the following exchange took place. '"Ah!

my pig", sayeth the King to him, for so he was wont to call him. "Yea", sayeth he, "if your Majesty had not been better to me than your bishops were, your pig had been roasted ere this time!"'

Dissent in these high circles was powerfully reinforced by the King's last marriage. Catherine's own learning has probably been exaggerated; so has her role as fairy stepmother who made all three of Henry's children one big happy family. What really mattered was her impact at court. As Queen, she had her own separate lodgings (often, in fact, the better half of the palace) and her own household. Some of her ladies were her own family connections; others were the wives of the King's Privy Chamber. Both groups were of the same religious complexion. Foxe singles out for special mention, 'as most of estimation and privy to all her doings', the Queen's sister, 'the Lady Herbert . . . and chief of her privy chamber, the Lady Lane, . . . her cousin . . ., [and] the Lady Tyrwhit'. To the list can be added women like Lady Denny and Lady Hoby, who not only shared their husbands' commitment but expressed it more openly. The Queen herself was with the foremost and the result was to make her Chamber a conventicle of the 'new' religion. It was not just a question of reading books, as with Anne Boleyn, but of public sermonizing. 'Every day in the afternoon for the space of an hour one of her chaplains, in her Privy Chamber, made some collation to her and to her ladies and gentlewomen of the Privy Chamber, or others that were disposed to hear.'

Among these 'others' were a number of the young gentlemen of the court. For the Reformation reflected the generation gap. To be young in the 1540s was to be 'new'; just as to be young in the 1960s was to be 'left'. The result was that immaculately conservative fathers could have hot-headed, radical sons. 'Mr Devereux, Lord Ferrers' son' questioned ancient rituals like creeping to the Cross and

Holy Water; while Lord Thomas Howard, son of the Duke of Norfolk himself, disputed 'indiscreetly of scripture with other young gentlemen of the court'. For such young men, Catherine's apartments provided both a forum and a sympathetic audience: when, for instance, during Lent 1546 the court preachers gave out the official conservative line, Lord Thomas vented his disagreement 'in the Queen's chamber and elsewhere in the court'.

The court, in a current phrase, was a 'beacon' to society. It was sending out some very strange signals and the conservatives made a determined attempt to stop them. In May 1546 the Imperial Ambassador noted that the Privy Council at Greenwich was 'busy against those suspected of forbidden opinions, which is a sign that the bishops and churchmen are more in favour'. Some soft targets, like Lord Thomas and his young friends at the court, were dealt with first. They escaped with a severe wigging, but rougher measures were used against leading dissenters in the clergy and City. And from there the net spread ever wider. Dr Huick, one of Henry's ever troublesome physicians, and John Lascelles, who had undone Catherine Howard five years before, were picked up for dissuading Dr Walter Crome, a leading radical preacher, from his recantation. Huick was broken by an investigation of his marital affairs; Lascelles finally went to the stake. Closely associated with Lascelles was the most impressive of the victims, Ann Ascue.

Ann was a young Lincolnshire gentlewoman whose husband had turned her out of his house for her advanced religious opinions. She then came to London and the attention of the authorities. She had been investigated in 1545 and got off with a dressing down. But this time there was no escape. In the middle of June she was summoned before the Privy Council at Greenwich and closely examined on two successive days about her views on the sacrament. After the second session, individual councillors continued to try to win her over to the Real Presence by fair words and foul. But she held firm and was sent back to London for trial and inevitable condemnation at the Guildhall.

Even then she was not left alone. She was a *cause célèbre*, and her recantation would have been an important propaganda victory. More important, people in high places had done what they could to comfort her in her imprisonment. The conservatives spotted their chance and on 29 June she was taken to the Tower. There the two chief legal experts on the Privy Council, Richard Rich and Thomas Wriothesley, made a ruthless attempt to extract the information they wanted. Were not high ladies of the court of her opinion? Could she not name 'a great number of my sect'? Were there not some of the Privy 'Council that did maintain me'? To all this she conceded nothing, save that her maid had told her that servants of the Countess of Hertford and Lady Denny had brought her money, but 'whether it were true or no, I cannot tell, for I am not sure who sent it me, but as the maid did say'. That was not enough, so she was racked; revived; then racked again. The Lieutenant of the Tower refused to perform the second torture; whereupon her interrogators, the Chancellor of the Court of Augmentations and the Lord Chancellor of England himself, 'throwing off their gowns, would needs play the tormentors themselves'.

This was breaking all the rules. Anne should have been protected against torture as a woman, as a gentlewoman, and as an already condemned person. Aware of their shaky ground, the Council was 'not a little displeased' that news of the racking spread, and the King himself was reported to be concerned. But the torture was the desperate act of desperate men. The conservative councillors thought that through Ann they could reach into the Privy Council, the

Queen's Privy Chamber and then who knows where. But her steadfastness confounded them. She was executed on 16 July 1546 at Smithfield. Her broken body was carried to the stake in a wooden chair, in which, still sitting, she was burned.

Indirect means having failed, the conservatives launched a direct attack on the Queen. This, thanks to some opportune leaking by another royal physician, Dr Wendy, and Catherine's own quick-thinking, was headed off and Henry and his Queen reconciled. Meanwhile, and all unaware of the turn of events, Wriothesley, Ann Ascue's torturer, arrived with a detachment of the Guard to arrest Catherine, only to find her and her ladies walking in the garden with Henry, who 'disposed himself to be as pleasant as ever he was in all his life before'. Wriothesley was driven from the presence with rude words: 'Arrant knave, beast and fool'.

During this time, Foxe explained, Henry 'lay at Whitehall, and used very seldom, being not well at ease, to stir out of his Chamber or Privy Gallery. And few of his Council, but by especial commandment, resorted until him.' This statement is confirmed at every point by contemporary sources. The attack on Catherine must have been planned in July 1546. On the 4th the Imperial Ambassador reported that 'the King has continued melancholy; . . . although dressed to go to mass, he did not go . . ., nor did he go into his garden as his habit is in the summer'. On the 6th he came to Whitehall from Greenwich, and was 'ill with colic'. And thereafter, for several days, the Privy Council shrank to the core of the conservative party. On 8 July, when a stringent proclamation against heretical books was issued, the attendance seems to have consisted only of Wriothesley, William Paulet, Lord St John, Gardiner, Anthony Browne and William Petre. These were religious conservatives to a man, as was the even smaller presence on the 10th of Wriothesley, Norfolk and Paulet.

Surrounded by this tight-knit group of politically motivated men, the pressure on Henry must have been intense. The only surprising thing is that Catherine eventually escaped. Henry, of course, had shut himself up before, during epidemics or at times of grief or crisis. But with his increasing ill-health periods of isolation became prolonged and frequent. For many years Henry had suffered from ulcers in first one and eventually both legs. These are usually supposed to be the result of syphilis. But there is no evidence for this. Henry's physicians were up-to-the-minute and would have administered mercury for venereal disease. His apothecary's accounts show that none was given, however. Instead, the ulceration could have been caused either by damaged and infected varicose veins, or (most likely) by fragments of bone broken off in a riding accident. The latter diagnosis would explain the characteristic cycle of illness: swelling and intense pain were followed by discharge and temporary relief. Save during these periods of intermission, exercise was difficult and the King put on weight rapidly. Which of course made things worse. By later 1546 he could scarcely walk and was carried 'to and fro in his galleries and chambers' in a pair of specially constructed 'chairs called trams', which were covered with quilted tawny velvet and embroidered with roses in Venice gold. And it was 'while passing' in one of these chairs in October 1546 that he had sent Secretary Paget with a message to the Imperial Ambassador.

So, immobile, in pain and frequently depressed, Henry was an ideal target for manipulation. But more was at stake than control of the present. Several times the acute phase of the cycle of his illness had brought Henry close to death, and on each occasion speculation and jockeying had risen to fever pitch. Faction bred in uncertainty, and a change of monarch was the greatest uncertainty of all.

Back in May 1538 a clot from his legs detached itself and lodged in his lungs. For several days he was speechless and black in the face. Death seemed inevitable and the Council split between those who wanted Mary to succeed and those who backed Edward. By the 1540s Edward's succession was no longer in doubt; instead the nature of the regency that would rule for him was the bone of contention. Around this all-important question politics realigned itself, making new alliances and breaking old friendships. A new world was in the offing, and a new generation was eager to take its place in it.

8

THE LAST MONTHS

Faction and the Future

ON SUNDAY, 16 January 1547, Mr Feckenham, chaplain to the Bishop of London, delivered a sermon at St Paul's Cross. Christ himself, St John the Baptist and Ezekiel, he insisted, were all more than thirty before they preached or bore witness, and Joseph and King David were also thirty years old before they bore rule. He then inveighed 'against the bringing up of youth of England in heresies, with oft exclamation, "Oh venerable senators and ancient fathers!" adding, "what a world shall it be when they shall have the rule, for if they have the swing it will be treason shortly to worship God"'.

The mid 1540s were a good time to be young. Henry himself, old and dying, still brooded over all like a baleful planet. But once more he was surrounded, as in the earlier days of the reign, with young men. Most were only to make their careers in the next reign. But one stands out: he burned like a meteor and burned out even before the old King was dead. This was Henry Howard, Earl of Surrey, eldest son of the Duke of Norfolk. Most early sixteenth-century Howards were dull dogs: hard, hard-nosed and dourly efficient. Surrey was quite different. There was something in him of his uncle Sir Edward, killed in action against the French in 1513, whose bold knight errantry and exaggerated chivalry had so attracted Henry VIII.

There was more, however, of the darker heredity of his maternal grandfather, Edward Stafford, last Duke of Buckingham. Surrey inherited all Buckingham's grand pride in blood and aristocracy, and all his determination that noblemen should once more come into their own. Perhaps it was from his mother's side too that he got his most dangerous trait: a rashness and a violence that bordered on madness. Add to all this an intelligence that was both penetrating and fast and the result was one of the most remarkable men of the age.

He was born in about 1517 and received an advanced education. John Clark was one of his teachers and as a mere boy he was making translations from Latin, Italian and Spanish. In 1529 he joined the household of the King's bastard son, the Duke of Richmond, and the two became close friends, both at home, at Windsor, where they spent most of their time, and abroad, at the court of Francis I, where they stayed as honoured guests for much of 1533. By birth, therefore, Surrey was an English nobleman. But by upbringing he was a prince, reared among princes; and by education and culture he was a complete cosmopolitan: he domesticated the Italian sonnet into English, and seems to have sat to the great Holbein more frequently than anyone else. The portrait sequence shows both the man's obsession with himself and his self-development, from the fresh-faced youth of 1532; through the rather uncertain young man of a few years later, to the set-piece portrait of about 1542. In the last he is dressed all in black; his eyes stare raptly into the distance, ignoring the spectator; and his left hand clutches his gown nervously to his breast. He is part poet, part malcontent.

Both aspects were reflected in the verse he wrote at Windsor in 1537. He had been confined there after he struck a fellow courtier in the gardens of Hampton Court, and in one poem in particular he recalled his earlier, happier stay at the castle with his friend the young Duke of Richmond. Life then was a perpetual round of dancing, hunting and sport; games and the game of love were delightfully interwoven and the tennis court became the court of Venus too:

The palm play were, despoyled [stripped] for the game,
With dazed eyes oft we by gleams of love
Have missed the ball and got sight of our dame,
To bait her eyes which kept the leads above.

Not much room for ideology, it would seem. But we would be wrong. Surrey and his mates were the elder brothers of the young men who disputed religion so hotly in Queen Catherine's chamber in the mid 1540s. There Lord Thomas Howard, his younger brother, had debated the authority of scripture and Surrey was hardly of the nature to have been left behind. Nor was he. One morning in early February 1543 London seethed with rumour. An armed band had wandered the city during the night, and there was 'great clamour of the breaking of glass windows, both of houses and churches, and shooting of men in the streets'. Surrey and his 'company' were identified as the culprits. They had lodged in the house of Millicent Arundel, where, it later transpired, they had also eaten flesh in Lent, and on Fridays and fast-days. The overtones of 'Protestantism' were clear, as was the element of straightforward vandalism and bravado. The following night Surrey was rebuked by his friend and fellow radical George Blage (the King's 'pig') and had the grace, rare in him, to admit that he had been wrong: 'he hath liever than all the good in the world it were undone, for he was sure it would come before the King and his Council; but we shall have a madding time in our youth, and therefore I am very sorry for it'.

Two or three years later a very different conversation

took place between Blage and the Earl. The subject was the composition of the regency government that would follow Henry VIII's death. Blage felt that 'such as the King should specially appoint thereto should be meetest to rule the Prince'; Surrey, on the other hand, held that 'his father was meetest both for good services done and for estate'. The disagreement quickly escalated into a violent quarrel, with Blage swearing that 'rather than it should come to pass that the Prince should be under the government of your father or you, I would bide the venture to thrust this dagger in you'.

Why had the two fallen out so completely? Several issues were involved. Blage, like anyone who knew Surrey well, would have felt that his tempestuous temperament unsuited him for power: he was fun as a friend; he would be deadly as a ruler. So, too, though for different reasons, would be his father the Duke. Blage loathed Norfolk's religious position and feared that under his guardianship 'the Prince should be but evil taught'. (It is probable too that Surrey, ever a weathercock, had by this time become as conservative as his father – his sister, the Duchess of Richmond, indeed asserted that he had always adhered to the old religion in his heart.) But underlying these questions of personality was a disagreement over fundamentals. When Blage asserted that the minority government should be corporate and nominated by the King, and when Surrey, on the contrary, insisted that it should be personal and depend on antiquity of lineage, they were reflecting two different concepts of political authority. Blage, the royal and official; Surrey, the narrowly aristocratic.

And Surrey maintained this view consistently and publicly. After Cromwell's death he had said to Sir Edmund Knyvet, whom he suspected of having benefited from the fallen minister's protection, 'Now is the false churl dead, so ambitious of others' blood. Now is he

stricken with his own staff.' Knyvet had replied, courage-
ously in the circumstances, that it was a sin to speak ill of
the dead. But Surrey had merely broadened the accusations
by saying, 'These new erected men would by their wills
leave no nobleman on life.' Norfolk himself held this view,
but discreetly. Surrey, on the other hand, who was
Buckingham's grandson as well as Norfolk's son, took the
high Stafford line and by his blatant and vehement
reiteration of it, gave many pause. More than Cromwell
were 'new erected' men at the court of Henry VIII; many
had even been erected by Cromwell. What would a
Norfolk regency mean for them? None could view the
prospect with anything but alarm, whether, like Blage, they
had been friends with Surrey, or whether, like Sir Anthony
Browne, they shared Norfolk's religious position.

But if the question of the regency divided and weakened
the 'old', it strengthened and united the 'new'. The 'new'
had reached its nadir in the summer of 1546. Under the
weight of the concerted conservative attack privy councillors like William Parr, Earl of Essex and Queen Catherine's
brother, and John Dudley, Viscount Lisle, had made a
show of joining in the attempt to win Ann Ascue to
orthodoxy. For their pains she had told them 'it was a great
shame for them to counsel contrary to their knowledge'.
To which they could only reply lamely 'that they would
gladly all things were well'. And even the Privy Chamber
had had its hands full to save Blage, who had been arrested
on 11 July – five days before Ann Ascue was burned. But
that had represented the high point of conservative success,
and thereafter there was a swift reversal of fortune.
Looking back in December 1546 the Imperial Ambassador
dated the change to the late summer. 'Four or five months
ago', he explained, 'was a great persecution of heretics and
sacramentalists, which has ceased since Hertford and the
Lord Admiral [Dudley] have resided at court.'

The two were visibly the men of the moment. John Dudley, son of the Edmund Dudley who had been executed at the beginning of Henry VIII's reign, had worked his passage back to favour and power. The reward came when, in the course of the single year 1542–3, he had been made a peer, a member of the Privy Chamber, Lord Admiral and a Privy Councillor. Edward Seymour's ascent had been even swifter, thanks to his sister's royal marriage and the birth of Prince Edward. Already Earl of Hertford, he had emerged in the campaigns of the 1540s – in obvious rivalry to Surrey – as England's most effective general. He and Dudley had been heavily involved in the concluding stages of the war with France, which had been going on since 1544. Hertford had been the King's lieutenant in Boulogne; Dudley had been one of the chief negotiators with France. That had kept them away from court, but peace in July allowed them to return and assume a leading role in events.

In itself their return can hardly have effected the political revolution noted by the Imperial Ambassador. But peace with France had had another and broader effect. Always foreign and domestic policy were intertwined. And the divorce and Reformation had only bound the links tighter. Charles V was the bastion of orthodoxy, just as he had been the defender of Catherine of Aragon. The only counterpoise to Charles was Francis I of France, who also, 'Most Christian' King that he was, wore his Catholicism more lightly than Charles. The result was that the swings back and forth of Henry's foreign and religious policies moved more-or-less together: the divorce and Reformation rested on alliance with France; while the moves towards orthodoxy in 1536, 1539–40 and again in the mid 1540s were associated either with a *rapprochement* with Charles or with actual alliance with him.

So it was in 1546. In pursuing a policy of peace with

France, Hertford and Dudley were following in the foot-steps of the ardently pro-French Anne Boleyn – for the same reasons and with not dissimilar results. Henry's reconciliation with Catherine Parr and the devastating rebuff of Wriothesley's attempt to arrest the Queen took place in the gardens of Hampton Court. Henry had gone there to preside over a magnificent welcome to d'Annebault, the Admiral of France, who had come to ratify the Anglo-French treaty in August 1546. Catherine's escape can thus be seen as the first fruits of the alliance; more was to follow. At the peak of the celebrations, in a specially erected pavilion, there took place an extra-ordinary conversation. Henry, leaning on the shoulders of Cranmer and the Admiral of France, explained that not only had the new allies decided to abolish papal authority in France, but also to change 'the mass in both realms into a communion service'.

Was Henry serious? Or was the remark merely part of his wilful double-dealing, with his own subjects and foreign powers alike? Who can say? But at least the incident was not isolated. Late the previous year Henry had appointed a committee chaired by Cranmer to look at religious ceremonial. The committee had reported in January 1546 and recommended the abolition of things like bell-ringing on Hallow'een. Henry agreed, and himself added kneeling to the Cross and the yet 'greater abuse of creeping to the Cross' on Good Friday to the list of banned customs. Only six years before, however, on Good Friday 1539, as the climax of an ostentatious display of con-ventional piety, 'the King's Grace crept to the Cross from the chapel door upward, devoutly, and so served the priest to mass that same day, his own person, kneeling on his Grace his knees'. For Henry now to repudiate what he had so recently practised was a revolution indeed. But it was an abortive one. For Gardiner, on a delicate embassy to the

Emperor, sent word that any further religious change at home would wreck the negotiations. The result was that when Denny brought the reforming orders to the King for signature, Henry refused, saying 'I am now otherwise resolved'. The strictly conditional nature of Henry's religious commitment was blatant. It was also taken for granted by the most advanced reformers themselves. In December 1546 John Hooper, afterwards Bishop of Gloucester, wrote from Basel to the great Continental reformer Bullinger of 'the good news' they had just received from other English exiles in Strasbourg. 'There will be a change of religion in England, and the King will take up the gospel of Christ if the Emperor be defeated in this most destructive war.' On the other hand, 'should the gospel sustain a loss, he will then retain his impious mass'.

Do we then abandon domestic history as a mere epiphenomenon, and write only of diplomacy and war? Not so, I think. For there is another side to the story. Gardiner, of course, was no neutral career diplomat, and when he had written as he did in January 1546 it is transparently clear that he was playing the foreign policy card to block religious change. Similarly, in December 1546 Hooper followed his brutally frank analysis of Henry's religious policy with an account of the great factional crisis at the English court which, as he well knew, had turned religion and politics upside-down. Policy – foreign, religious, domestic – was ultimately decided by the King. But in that 'ultimately' is a whole world of political manoeuvre. There was an art, as both Gardiner and his opponents knew, in moulding the King's decisions, and there was an art too in turning those decisions to one's own advantage. The events of July and August meant that the wind was blowing favourably for the 'new'. But that the wind turned into a gale which blew away the 'old' and uprooted the great house of Howard was a work of political art.

The artist, the magician that conjured the wind, was William Paget, the royal Secretary and the shrewdest politician on the Council. Known as the 'master of practices', he was a natural 'politique'. Or, as Bishop Ponet put it less kindly, he 'will have one part in every pageant, if he may by praying or paying put in his foot'. In the summer of 1546 he had appeared as a leader of the conservatives, and the Imperial Ambassador had more than once reported him resolute against the 'Protestants'. At the same time, however, he had cast himself as Hertford's principal political adviser. He did so on the simplest grounds of expediency. He could have worked with a Howard regency just as well but he calculated (wrongly in the event) that Hertford would be easier to manage. First, however, Hertford had to be got into power. Against that event there were formidable obstacles: not only the conservative majority in the Privy Council but also the power of the Howards and the intelligence of Bishop Gardiner of Winchester. And Gardiner, 'the doctor of practices', was more committed than Paget but scarcely less able as a manoeuvrer of men. Paget's mind, though, was equal to the challenge and he spotted that the key lay in the Privy Chamber.

As long ago as 1545, in a letter giving Hertford sound advice on how to manage the complex and variable structures of the court, Paget had recommended that 'your lordship shall do well to salute now and then, with a word or two in a letter, my Lord of Suffolk and my Lord Wriothesley and such others as you shall think good; forgetting not Mr Denny'. Denny was not forgotten, and an alliance was quickly cemented. It appears only fitfully in correspondence: after all its deliberations were probably better not written down. But its practical effects are unmistakable. In September 1546 it was clear to all observers that something was stirring: 'great activity is still displayed against sectarians, but the results are not so satisfactory as at first', noted the Imperial Ambassador. More ominously, he added, 'there are people here trying to get into favour who will not suit our purpose'. He was desperate to have an audience with the King to assess at first hand 'what is going on'. Later in the month the answer became clearer. Henry fell dangerously ill again, 'and the physicians gave little hope of his recovery'. The competitors for power reacted in two different ways. Norfolk and Surrey talked openly – too openly – of a Howard regime under Edward; while their opponents methodically consolidated their grip on power in preparation for the next, and as it must have seemed to everybody, final crisis in the King's health.

The 'new' were already very strong in the Privy Chamber. But there was an important loophole. For though Denny headed the largest faction in the Privy Chamber; controlled the administrative machinery of the Privy Coffers and Dry Stamp and stood highest in the royal favour, he was only one of a duumvirate, and the junior half at that. He was second Chief Gentleman of the Privy Chamber; the first Chief Gentleman and Groom of the Stool was Sir Thomas Heneage. For the full potential of the Chief Gentlemanship to be unlocked, the two had to work as one. Heneage (Cromwellian appointee that he was) was probably not unsympathetic to the 'new', but he was no partisan. In the circumstances that was not enough and in October 1546 – despite twenty years' service and his evident chagrin – he was dismissed. Denny stepped into his shoes and in Denny's old place as second-in-command of the Privy Chamber was put Sir William Herbert, Catherine Parr's brother-in-law. The perfect partnership at the head of the Privy Chamber was forged.

Secure now at court, the 'new', hitherto on the defensive, moved into the attack. The first victim was Gardiner. He was manoeuvred into a trumped-up quarrel with the King over an exchange of lands. Invariably his technique in a tight corner had been to seek a personal interview with the King. That had saved him before, but this time it was denied. 'Such as come now to the court were specially sent for'; he, on the other hand, had 'no such opportunity to make humble suit to your highness's presence'. Desperately he wrote to Henry on 2 December, begging for an audience. Back came the devastating reply: the King saw 'no cause why you should molest us further', as the surrender of the lands, which Gardiner professed himself willing to make, could be performed to the King's officials in London. The language of the letter sounds like Henry's, but it was signed with the stamp 'in presence of Anthony Denny, Knight and John Gates, Esquire'; while with Denny and Herbert in firm control of the entrée to the Privy Chamber, there was no question of Gardiner's 'friends in the Privy Chamber' getting him to the King up the back stairs, as they once would have done.

The 'new' now struck even higher. On 2 December, the day Gardiner wrote to Henry begging the audience that was so rudely denied, Sir Richard Southwell informed the Privy Council 'that he knew certain things of the Earl [of Surrey] that touched his fidelity to the King'. In his usual fashion Surrey offered to vindicate himself by fighting Southwell in his shirt. His offer was not taken up; instead both were committed to custody while the charges were investigated. On the 3rd and 4th, Norfolk, who was in the country, wrote to friends in London, and particularly Gardiner, to find out the cause of his son's arrest. They, of course, had been neutralized already, and in any case the letters probably fell into the hands of the Council. Meanwhile the Council was going through the Earl's circle of bright but quarrelsome young men with a toothcomb. By Sunday, 12 December, they had discovered enough. In the morning Surrey was transferred from Wriothesley's house at Ely Palace to the Tower; then Norfolk, who had just come up to London, was stripped of his Treasurer's staff and the Garter and sent to the Tower in his turn; and finally, between 3 and 4 pm, a party of three horsemen and their servants left the Council to ride off to take possession of the Duke's houses and lands. In charge was the strong man of the Privy Chamber, John Gates, who was accompanied by his and Denny's brother-in-law, Sir Wymond Carew, and, of all people, Surrey's original accuser Sir Richard Southwell. The smell of both vendetta and put-up job is very strong. The party reached Kenninghall, the Duke's principal house, at daybreak on the 14th: papers and valuables were seized; the household broken up; and the Duke's daughter, the Dowager Duchess of Richmond and his mistress, Elizabeth Holland, prepared for their journey to London and their confrontation with the Council. They found, Gates and the rest reported next day, a 'frank disposition' in the Duchess.

Everyone else involved showed the same. The result was that the government uncovered everything, from Surrey's arrogance and his disdain for the King's humbly-born councillors, to his determination to have a Howard-dominated government during Edward's minority. Other things, equally damaging if not more so, came out as well, like his suggestion to his sister, Mary of Richmond, that she should make herself the King's mistress. The occasion had been the scheme, floated by Norfolk the previous June, for a family compact between the Howards and the Seymours. The Duchess Mary had not been struck with her share of the bargain, which was to be a marriage with the egregious Sir Thomas Seymour. Only let her dissemble, however, advised Surrey, and when she was interviewed by the King about the marriage, she might take Henry's fancy, 'whereby in process she should bear as great a stroke about him as Mme d'Etampes doth about the French King'.

Finally, it transpired, his price of blood had led him to dangerous heraldic display. Of royal descent on both sides, he had incorporated the arms of Edward the Confessor into his own, and had marshalled the shields of other royal ancestors in the heraldic glass of his houses.

A summary of all the charges was drawn up and amended by Henry in his own hand. The writing is tremulous, but the eye for detail is as sharp and pedantic as ever. All the points of substance appeared in the paper, but the King and his advisers decided to indict Surrey only on the heraldic charge (the others were probably too embarrassing politically). The trial took place on 13 January 1547. Surrey made a characteristically swashbuckling defence, but was found guilty and executed six days later. His father had wisely thrown the towel in much earlier. The day after his arrest he had offered to surrender lands and goods to the King; and on 12 January he made a formal confession of his guilt in concealing his son's treason (thereby, of course, prejudicing Surrey's trial the following day). Parliament passed a bill of attainder on father and son, to which the royal assent was given by commission (signed with the stamp of course) on 27 January. That night Henry died, and his death saved Norfolk's life.

By the standards of the age, Surrey's guilt, if not his father's, was well established. But the pair were still victims of a conspiracy. The Imperial Ambassador considered that 'this misfortune to the house of Norfolk may have come from that quarter', by which he meant Hertford and Dudley. And it is clear that Surrey saw even further. In a paper of memoranda culled from the various interrogations appears this note: 'things in common: Paget, Hertford, Admiral, Denny'. Too late Surrey had understood the forces that had come together to destroy him; and too late also he had been working to break up the coalition. Another of these memoranda reads 'that Mr P. should be Chancellor of England'. To have detached Paget from Hertford six months earlier would have changed everything. Now, however, Paget was to achieve his master-stroke for the other side.

The muzzling of Gardiner and the destruction of the Howards was only the negative side of the coup engineered by the 'new'. Their positive aims were pretty widely guessed at as well and on 24 December the Imperial Ambassador reported that 'it is even asserted that the custody of the Prince and the government of the realm will be entrusted to them' (i.e. Hertford and Dudley). By the Act of Succession of 1536 the arrangements for both the succession and the minority government would be settled by Henry's will. The will, hastily written on paper, with blanks and corrections, and once contained in a 'round box or bag of black velvet', is one of the most intriguing, and intrigued over, documents in English history. Under Elizabeth I it was kept in a special iron chest in the Treasury, along with another 'leather bag with diverse secret writings in the same, which is not to be opened but by the Council'.

The man who had the key to these secrets was Paget. Before Parliament he did 'say and affirm on his honour that he was privy to the beginning, proceeding and ending of the same last will', and, in private conversation with the great jurist Edmund Plowden, he went further and said that 'he wrote the will himself or first draft thereof'.

At first sight, to be sure, the will seems straightforward enough. Henry begins with a rather heterodox confession of his faith, and goes on to provide generously for the burial of his body in this world and the salvation of his soul in the next. Then the succession is settled on his children, Edward, Mary and Elizabeth in that order, and in default of their heirs on the descendants of his younger sister Mary and his old friend Charles Brandon, Duke of Suffolk. This meant that the 'foreign' line of his elder sister Margaret, who had married James IV of Scotland, was excluded (and this in turn is why the will became such a hot potato under Elizabeth). Next provision was made for the minority of Edward. All power, 'public and private', was to be in the hands of a Council of sixteen executors. Their role was envisaged as strictly corporate: none of them was 'to presume to meddle with our treasure, or to do anything appointed by our will alone'. As far as the King could make sure, it would seem, there was to be no wicked uncle, no Richard of Gloucester to undo what Henry VIII and his father had achieved. Finally, generous cash legacies were left to his executors, and other councillors and servants. The whole will was then 'signed . . . with our hand, in our Palace of Westminster, the 30th day December' 1546, in the presence of ten witnesses whose signatures follow.

The first and key problem is with the dating clause itself. For the will was not signed but stamped with the Dry Stamp. Nor was the stamp even applied on the day stated. In the monthly schedules of documents stamped which Clerk drew up, the will appears as the next-to-last item for *January* 1547, just before the commission to give the assent to Norfolk's Act of Attainder. The original of the commission is dated 27 January, which was the last day of the King's life. It is just possible that the will entry was placed here by 'innocent mistake', though bearing in mind the importance of the document the mistake is a rum one. However, powerful and persistent tradition insisted that the will had been stamped only 'when the King himself was new dead, or dying and past all remembrance'. And the tradition is corroborated by incontrovertible evidence that the actual contents of the will were altered long after the date on which it was supposed to have been signed. Sir Thomas Seymour was listed as a councillor in the will, but he was only appointed to the Privy Council on 23 January. An even later date is suggested by Dudley's account of the same episode: Henry, he said (according to Foxe), 'being on his deathbed, and hearing [Seymour's] name among those elected to the Council, cried out "no, no!", though his breath was failing him'. The same tell-tale reference to Henry's deathbed appears in Paget's testimony, recorded in the Privy Council register within days of the event, that the King, 'being remembered in his deathbed that he had promised great things to divers men . . . willed in his testament that whatever should in any wise appear to his Council to have been promised by him, the same should be performed'.

Armed with this sort of evidence, no modern court would hesitate to overturn Henry's last will and testament. Our task is to explain, however. One view sees the chicanery as part of Henry's ruthless game of divide and rule with his ministers. The completed but unsigned will was a sword of Damocles over their heads: one false move and they were out. I am sceptical. If this were Henry's intention, would not a signed will and the threat of a codicil have been more effective? And in any case, as we have shown, not only was the will unsigned till the King's deathbed, its contents were substantially changed, or even determined, then as well. That cannot have been part of the King's game with his servants; it must have been part of their game with each other. And the stake was not the ebbing authority of the old King, but the power to speak in the name of the new.

The apparently immovable obstacle to such a view of the will has always been the clause forbidding any one councillor to act alone. Hertford's goal was to be Protector; how could he have engineered a will that expressly forbade a protectorate? Once again, however, the clause is not what it seems. Individual action by a single councillor was indeed excluded, but not if 'the most part of the whole number of their co-executors do consent and by writing agree to the same'. This condition stands things on their head: it makes the clause forbidding the protectorate into the machinery for creating a protectorate. And it was so used. On 4 February the Council of Executors gathered together and considered whether, though the will had given them all 'like and equal charge', it would not be better 'that some special man . . . should be prepared in name and place before others'. They decided that it would. 'We therefore by one whole assent, concord and agreement . . . have given unto [Hertford] the name and title of . . . Protector . . . and of . . . Governor of [the King's] most royal person.' They claimed to be acting 'by virtue of the authority' of the will, and indeed they had followed the procedures it laid down to the letter: Hertford was appointed by 'the most part' (thirteen out of sixteen) of the executors; and their consent was confirmed 'by writing' their signatures to the act in the Privy Council register.

But before this machinery could be put into motion, Hertford had to be confident of the backing of a majority of the Council. That he had never had in the old Privy Council; instead, as the persecutions of 1546 showed, Gardiner could command a majority in any reasonably full meeting of the board. The will changed that too, and by the most outrageous gerrymandering. The Privy Council of Henry's last years had numbered just over twenty; the Council of Executors consisted of sixteen. But only ten of these were carried over from the existing Privy Council. The newcomers fell into three pairs: Denny and Herbert, the court leaders of the 'new'; the Wotton brothers who were absent in France throughout; and two judges, one of whom appears to have been weak in the head and never attended. Excluding these makeweights, therefore, the working council numbered only thirteen, in which the 'new' commanded for the first time a safe majority. The twelve members of the Privy Council who were excluded from the Council of Executors were constituted into a second-string 'Council for the aiding and assisting of the . . . executors'. The arrangement was bizarre, divisive, and short-lived. Once the crucial business of 'electing' Hertford Protector was out of the way, the two groups were quickly reunited into a single, though of course much enlarged, Privy Council.

The short-lived expedient of the two Councils is typical of the will as a whole. Its most important clauses are best explained as minimal and subtle forgeries, conceived and executed by Paget, and designed to further the interests of the 'new' in general and Hertford in particular. Why should this extraordinary action have been necessary? We can only guess. Perhaps Henry had not yet fully come round to their way of thinking. Perhaps, more likely, he had signed a will on 30 December, in the presence of the ten named witnesses. If so, it was not the text we have; nor had the witnesses signed what they thought. They could well have written in fact on a blank sheet, for the last lines of the will are written more closely together, as though the signatures were already there. It was by no means satisfactory (Hertford strongly advised against publishing any more than the bare minimum of the text). And clearly it had all been a rush, with important details still being thrashed out as the King was dying and just afterwards. 'Remember', Paget later wrote to Hertford, 'what you promised me in the gallery at Westminster, before the breath was out of the body of the King that dead is. Remember what you promised me immediately after, devising with me concerning the place which you now occupy.'

Paget deserved Hertford's promise (which the Protector conspicuously failed to keep). But if Paget were the brains behind the affair, what made it possible was the 'new's' control of the Privy Chamber. The original will had been in Denny's keeping; while the stamp, the sole instrument by which the will was authenticated, was his to apply as required. Finally and above all there was the entrée to the Privy Chamber, the regulation of which was shared by Denny and Herbert. From the beginning of December they used this power ruthlessly to close the Privy Chamber to all but a handful of 'Councillors and three or four Gentlemen of the Chamber'. No unwelcome influence could reach the King; nor could anyone contradict whatever stories of Henry's last hours they put around. This hermetical seal on access to the King was the precondition for the 'new's' whole management of the events of December and January; it was also put to highly specific use to activate perhaps the strangest clause of this strange will.

This we have touched on briefly with Paget's description of the last-minute inclusion in the will of an 'unfulfilled gifts clause'. This provided that whatever gifts or grants Henry had promised but not yet performed at the time of his death should be carried out by his executors. The only condition was that the gifts 'shall appear to our said Executors . . . to have been granted or promised by us in any manner wise'. It does seem clear that, in his last weeks and flush with the seizure of the Norfolk inheritance, Henry had been talking of a mass promotion of his councillors and favourites to the peerage, and an equally massive distribution of royal lands. But how far arrangements had gone we cannot be sure. What is certain, however, is the use to which the 'unfulfilled gifts clause' was put. A joint 'declaration' of the King's intentions was drawn up by Paget, Denny and Herbert. Paget, explaining 'as is well known' that Henry 'used to open his pleasure to me alone in many things', set out the supposed arrangements in detail; they were then confirmed by Denny and

Herbert, who explained in turn that Henry 'would always when Mr Secretary [Paget] was gone tell us what had happened between them as well in that matter as for the most part in all other things'. Even in this declaration the shameless back-scratching of the alliance stands out. Paget claimed to have pressed the King particularly hard for Denny, since he 'had divers times been a suitor for me and I never for him'; while Denny and Herbert, on the other hand, had reminded Henry that Paget 'had well remembered all men saving one'. To which Henry had replied, 'you mean himself', and given Paget as much as Herbert! On the basis of such assertions only, a duke, a marquess, two earls and four barons were created, and £3200 *per annum* (at a very conservative valuation) of Crown lands given away. The 'new' had gained power with the will; with the operation of the 'unfulfilled gifts clause' they obtained status and power too. They also had the sense to use the distribution of titles and land to buy the acquiescence, or at least the silence, of their surviving opponents as well.

In this dissection of faction and self-interest the actual events of Henry's last weeks have been passed over. This is inevitable, since we, no more than contemporaries, cannot pass beyond Denny and Herbert at the door of the Privy Chamber. There is rumour, and the odd nugget of firm information; otherwise only what they chose to tell. On 8 January the French Ambassador noted that the 'King has been so ill for the past fifteen days that he was reported dead'. And many, he added, 'still believe him so, seeing that, whatever amendment is announced, few persons have access to his lodgings and his chamber'. On 17 January, however, Henry was sufficiently recovered to receive both the French and Imperial Ambassadors. Gracefully he apologized for the fact that his indisposition had prevented the speedy dispatch of their business. That was the last time than any neutral party saw Henry.

Ten days later came the end. Foxe makes an edifying scene of it. Henry's physicians despaired of the King's life, but dared not tell him. So Denny, 'boldly coming to the King', told Henry of his state and 'exhorted him to prepare himself to death'. For the last time the rhetoric of the courtier was turned on him, and, as so often, it half won Henry over. Denny then asked Henry if he wanted to speak with any 'learned man'; Henry replied 'that if he had any, it should be Dr Cranmer'. Should he be sent for? pursued Denny. 'I will first', said the King, 'take a little sleep, and then as I feel myself, I will advise upon the matter.' They were his last words. He had so often put off a decision thus before; this time he delayed too long. He regained consciousness but was past speech. All he could do was clutch Cranmer's hand as the Archbishop, who had been sent for post-haste, spoke to him reassuringly of salvation in Christ.

This last dying gesture became a kind of laying-on of hands. By it the King who had broken the bonds of Rome seemed to confer his blessing on the new, Protestant English Church that Cranmer, more than anyone else, was to create under Edward VI. By an equally slender gesture, we may guess, the King was brought to agree to his will. The will was read, stamped and sealed. Then, in dumb show, the King was made to hand his testament – and the future – to Hertford. Did he know what he did? Did he know what was in the will? God alone knows.

Nor by then did it really matter. The key to the future was the will, already enclosed in its black velvet box. And the key to the box was held by Hertford. At two o'clock in the morning of 28 January Henry died. But none beyond the palace was any the wiser. After further hasty consultations Hertford and Sir Anthony Browne, the Master of the Horse, rode to Prince Edward who was lodged at

Hertford. And only on the 29th, once the Prince was safely in his hands, did the Earl send the key of the will to Paget. And only two days later, on 31 January, when Edward had been brought to the Tower, did the heralds proclaim: 'The King is dead; long live the King!'

Henry VIII's will, in short, is the epitome of his reign. Far from being the King's attempt to prolong his rule beyond the grave, as most historians have supposed, its essential features were determined by other intelligences and shaped for other purposes. The *persona* of Henry VIII has cast a powerful spell on both contemporaries and succeeding generations, but, as in the original sense of the word, the *persona* was a mask through which spoke the King's servants more often than the King himself.

The realization is an uncomfortable one, since it means that the obscenities of the reign, and there were many, can no longer be dismissed as the actions of an all-powerful tyrant. Rather, like the regime itself, they were a corporate responsibility. For in the circle of manipulators were the most distinguished of the English governing class. And what was done in Henry VIII's name was their doing as much as his. This in turn makes moral judgement (unless, like W. G. Hoskins's, it be a searing condemnation of the entire reign as *An Age of Plunder*) meaningless. There are no villains and no victims. Or rather, the wheel of fortune turns men from one into the other: the trials of Exeter and Carew were rigged, but then they had helped to arrange the same fate for Anne Boleyn and her supporters; Cromwell's execution was horribly unjust, but he had sent both the Boleyns and Exeter and his friends to their deaths; while Norfolk, who engineered Cromwell's fall, was himself brought down seven years later. It is true, of course, that it was the peculiarities of the King's character that made both the rewards and the penalties of politics so great. But only a few isolated figures like More or Wyatt quarrelled, and then only on paper, with the resulting rules of the game, and even they, when they had the opportunity, played as dirtily as the rest.

BIBLIOGRAPHY

Except where otherwise printed the place of publication is London

My principal source, like that of every other historian of the reign, has been *Letters and Papers, Foreign and Domestic, of the Reign of Henry VIII, 1509–47*, ed., J. S. Brewer, *et al.* (1862–1932). This has been my bible for more years than I care to remember. But in writing this book I discovered the Prefaces, and have pillaged both their material and their judgements ruthlessly.

1 THE NATURE OF POLITICS

Henry VIII's personality was complex enough, and the sources are ambiguous enough, for there to be a wide range of views of his character. Three contrasting interpretations are: G. R. Elton, *Reform and Reformation* (1977), J. J. Scarisbrick, *Henry VIII* (1968) and L. B. Smith, *Henry VIII: the Mask of Royalty* (1971). Religious developments are almost as disputed as the King's character, and a good, though itself tendentious, guide is Christopher Haigh, 'The Recent Historiography of the English Reformation', *Historical Journal* 25 (1982). The reign of Henry VII is less well served and there is no satisfactory modern life. Best is R. L. Storey, *The Reign of Henry VII* (1968). Develop-

146

ments in the court and politics are sketched in G. R. Elton, 'Tudor Government: the points of contact; III: the Court', *Transactions of the Royal Historical Society* (1976) and David Starkey, 'The Age of the Household', in Stephen Medcalf, *The Later Middle Ages* (1981). Faction, the latest buzz-word among early-modern historians, is discussed in E. W. Ives, *Faction in Tudor England* (Historical Association Pamphlet, 1979) and David Starkey, 'From Feud to Faction', *History Today* 32 (1982); while David Starkey, 'The Court: Castiglione's ideal and Tudor reality', *Journal of the Warburg and Courtauld Institutes* 45 (1982) gives a political interpretation of *The Courtier*.

2 A NEW AGE

A good discussion of the 'noble reaction' at the beginning of Henry VIII's reign is R. L. Storey, *Henry VII*. More's part in the affair is dealt with by Richard Marius, *Thomas More* (1985). For the kind of views on Henry VIII's relations with his family and nobility that are taken issue with in the text see for example M. Levine, *Tudor Dynastic Problems, 1460–1571* (1973) and G. W. Bernard, *The Power of the Early Tudor Nobility* (Brighton, 1985). C. G. Cruickshank, *Army Royal* (Oxford, 1969) is a straightforward account of the French campaign of 1513.

3 THE CARDINAL

Rehabilitation of Wolsey after the attacks of A. F. Pollard, *Wolsey* (1965) and G. R. Elton, *England under the Tudors* (1953) was begun by J. J. Scarisbrick, *Henry VIII* and continued, from a different perspective, by Peter Gwyn, 'Wolsey's Foreign Policy: the conferences at Bruges and Calais', *Historical Journal* 23 (1980). Both sides of the debate devalue the perceptive account of Wolsey's style given by the man best placed to know, his gentleman usher, George Cavendish, in R. S. Sylvester and D. P. Harding, eds., *Two Early Tudor Lives* (New Haven and London, 1962). Important and unused material about Wolsey's handling of the Great Seal is in the Hanaper accounts, especially Public Record Office, E101/221/9, mm 2v and 5.

4 THE COURT AND THE CARDINAL
There is no proper biographical material on Carew or Bryan, but the lives in S. T. Bindoff, ed., *The History of Parliament: the House of Commons, 1509–58* (1983) are a start. However, they rather fail to grasp the excitement of either the men or their times and for that the reader should turn if possible to Bryan's own brilliant translation of Antonio de Guevara, *A Dispraise of the Life of the Courtier and a Commendation of the Life of the Labouring Man* (1548). The account of the development of the Privy Chamber and its relations with Wolsey follows in the main David Starkey, 'The King's Privy Chamber, 1485–1547' (unpublished Cambridge PhD dissertation, 1973), but for 1517 I have added the important letter book in Bodley, Ashmole MS 1148 article XI. My account of the fall of the Duke of Buckingham is based directly on the material in *Letters and Papers*, and differs from E. W. Ives, *Faction in Tudor England* in presenting Buckingham as a loner rather than as the head of a court faction.

5 ANNE BOLEYN
The career of Anne Boleyn is undergoing important and long overdue reassessment. Hugh Paget, 'The Youth of Anne Boleyn', *Bulletin of the Institute of Historical Research* (1982) sorts out her early years; while Maria Dowling, 'Scholarship, Politics and the Court of Henry VIII' (unpublished London PhD dissertation, 1981) sets her religion and patronage in a clearer light. I have drawn on both heavily.

6 THOMAS CROMWELL

The presentation of Thomas Cromwell as a dominant figure of early sixteenth-century history has been the outstanding achievement of Professor G. R. Elton. Elton himself has described Cromwell the administrator in *The Tudor Revolution in Government* (Cambridge, 1953), and the social reformer in *Reform and Renewal* (Cambridge, 1973). My own work emphasizes rather Cromwell the brilliant but religiously-committed politician. Professor Elton took much of this on board in *Reform and Reformation*, but the present chapter offers a fuller statement of my views.

7 THE LAST YEARS

The evidence of Henry VIII's last years is the most complex and hardest to interpret of the whole reign. On the Privy Council, I am arguing against G. R. Elton, *The Tudor Revolution in Government*, and on politics, against L. B. Smith, *The Mask of Royalty*. On politics, it is simply a different reading of the same sources, in particular, J. Foxe, *Acts and Monuments*, ed., J. Pratt (1874); on the Privy Council, I attach novel importance to the two acts of Parliament of 1539–40 (31 Henry VIII, c.8 and c.10) which between them effectively redefined both nobility and conciliar office. And, as throughout, the role of the Privy Chamber provides a fresh means of articulating the narrative.

8 THE LAST MONTHS

This chapter hinges round my interpretation of Henry VIII's will. Its main lines are summarized in G. R. Elton, *Reform and Reformation*; while Helen Miller, 'Henry VIII's unwritten will', in E. W. Ives *et al.*, ed., *Wealth and Power in Tudor England* (1978), complements and confirms.

INDEX